DREAMS ABOUT THE DEAD

Glimpses of Grief

Dennis Raymond Ryan

D1520312

University Press of America,® Inc.
Lanham · Boulder · New York · Toronto · Oxford

Copyright © 2006 by
University Press of America,® Inc.
4501 Forbes Boulevard
Suite 200
Lanham, Maryland 20706
UPA Acquisitions Department (301) 459-3366

PO Box 317
Oxford
OX2 9RU, UK

Library of Congress Control Number: 2006923757
ISBN-13: 978-0-7618-3496-0 (paperback : alk. paper)
ISBN-10: 0-7618-3496-6 (paperback : alk. paper)

For my wife, Judy

Table of Contents

Preface

This book had its roots in the death of my first son, Raymond. He died during my first year of teaching Religious Studies at the College of New Rochelle. He was only two weeks old. My wife, Judy, and I were deeply affected. I tried to cope by reading everything I could about the grief we were experiencing. I wanted to understand what was happening to us. What I found was fascinating and helpful. Less than a year later, my older sister, Marcia, died suddenly from a cerebral hemorrhage. She left behind my brother-in-law and their five-year-old daughter, Cristina. This was another painful death for our family, but what I had learned helped us avoid unnecessary pain. I continued to study about grief. In my college teaching, I was aware that many students were being affected by death, so I obtained permission to teach a new course, "Death, Grief and Religion."

From time to time, students in the course asked me the meaning of dreams they had about dead relatives and friends. I didn't know how to answer them, so I began to study about dreams. I learned two things that influenced the direction I took with the students. First, the most important interpretation of a dream is the one the dreamer discovers for herself. Second, questions about the dream help the dreamers find the meaning that makes sense to them. So I made up a list of questions to ask the students about their dreams. Almost all the students found the questions helpful in finding a meaning for their dreams.

I found the interviews revealing and began using excerpts in class to illustrate elements of grief. The interviews revealed six elements of grief. There were the memories of the deceased. There were fantasies about them. There were the emotional responses and the cognitive responses to the death. There were the insights about the relationship and about life. Finally, there were their beliefs that a real transformation had occurred and that the deceased continued to exist in a spiritual realm.

At some point, some students asked me if I were writing a book about these dreams. I decided I would, but I wanted to wait until I had collected over one thousand interviews. It took many years, but now I think I have a representative sample of such dreams.

I want to thank my students, many of whom are the subjects in the study. I thank them for their openness, their willingness to help, and their encouragement. I want to thank my wife and son and daughter for their encouragement and for accepting all the time I spent working on the book and not with them. I want to thank my colleagues at the College of New Rochelle, for their encouragement and suggestions, especially Jim Magee, Rosemarie Hurrell, and Ken Doka.

Dennis Ryan
New Rochelle, New York
December 15, 2005

Chapter 1: The Study

Stephanie was an eighteen-year-old college student at the time of the interview. She had recently dreamed of her grandfather the day after he died. Here's part of what she said.

> I was home and looked outside. It was sunny and bright and I felt wonderful. Then I saw my grandfather standing at the bottom of the driveway. I went out the front door and ran down to him. Now it was no longer like a dream but like it was really happening. I asked him what he was doing here since he was dead. He told me he was going away but would see me again. We hugged and said goodbye and I woke up.
>
> I felt like I really saw him, really spoke to him, but I was confused. Most of the time I know when I am dreaming but this was very real. It made me think about dreaming in general. I think that dreams happen because of what's going on in our lives. They are everything that's in our mind put together and we make up our own dreams. But this didn't seem like one of those dreams. It was different. The dream showed me how close we were and answered my question if he was okay.

No one knows how many people, like Stephanie, dream about dead loved ones, but it seems as if everyone knows at least one person who has had such a dream. These are usually vivid, powerful experiences that are remembered for a long time. This book is filled with excerpts of interviews with subjects like Stephanie.

Stephanie talked about being confused because her dream experience was different from what she had learned about dreams. Let's look briefly at some ideas about dreams.

Understanding dreams

Dreams are experiences we have while asleep. They seem more or less real to us while they are taking place. Some are pleasant; others are not. Everyone dreams, but some people never recall dreaming. No one recalls every dream and, in general, dreams are very easily forgotten. There are, however, dreams that are so vivid that they are remembered years after the dream experience. Dreams are usually like a story. The dreamer either takes part in the story, or merely observes what happens. Sometimes the dreamer, like Stephanie, realizes she is dreaming and alters what happens in the dream. This is called a "lucid" dream.[1] There are a couple of examples in this book. Most of the dreams were vivid, that is very realistic, but not "lucid."

Stephanie also learned that dreams are connected to "what's going on in our lives." Dreams are usually images that relate to our waking world but are different or changed in some way. This is called the continuity theory about dreams and is widely accepted. Historical evidence indicates humans have been wondering about dreams since, at least, ancient Assyria and Babylonia.[2] Many theories about dreams have been developed as well as dream manuals. Today, many of these interpretations continue to compete for acceptance.[3]

Some dreamers in the study had learned something about interpreting dreams and some used what they knew to interpret their dream. For example, Gerri was a dreamer who used a dream book to help her understand her dream. She was eighteen years old and her friend died of leukemia when they were both seventeen. She had the dream almost a week after the death.

In the dream, I was living in an apartment. It was very bright in the apartment when the phone rang. I answered and it was my mother and we started to talk. Then I got a beep (I have call waiting), so I switched over to the other line, and it was my dead friend Mark. So I flashed back to the other line, and I told my mom that it was Mark, and she said, "Mark who?" I said his full name and she said, "But he's dead," and I said, "I know. Bye!" and I hung up. I flashed back over to the other line. The apartment was getting brighter, but his voice was muffled. I knew it was him, but I really couldn't hear him clearly. He said my name and asked, "Is that you?" and I asked, "Mark, is that you?" Then he said, "Yeah. Hi!" I asked him how he was and he said, "I'm fine, but I'm bleeding. I'm bleeding." That made me very nervous, and I wanted to hang up and was trying to hang up but was fascinated. He kept saying, "I'm fine, but I'm bleeding." Then he said, "I'm in London." Then I was really freaked out and slammed down the phone.

When I woke up, I had this really weird feeling. I was really scared because I didn't understand what bleeding meant, so I looked it up in a dream book I have and it said that bleeding means death. But Mark also said he was fine, so I was confused. I believe that he was trying to say that even though he was dead, he was fine. The part about being in London I took as meaning that he was free now and his spirit could go wherever he wanted. The dream really made me think. You know how people say, "Today was such a waste of a day?" Well, I correct myself now when I'm about to say that, because I realize that no matter how bad your day was, you have to be thankful that you at least had a day. Some people didn't get the opportunity to see another day. I honestly think about this all the time now. I believe he was letting me know that he was okay.

Gerri used a dream manual but ultimately she discovered a meaning that made sense to her. Many psychologists think that this is most important. Louis LaGrand wrote, "No one has a universal answer to explain dreams; it's good to consider alternate explanations, but it remains the right of the dreamer to decide how to interpret it."[4]

Some psychologists propose that dreams are products of the subconscious or the unconscious. Sigmund Freud thought dreams were disguised wish-fulfillments.[5] Carl Jung wrote that dreams were means of integrating the conscious part of the self with the unconscious part.[6] Calvin Hall asserted that dreams were images that embodied thoughts; he used content analysis to uncover a dreamer's personal thoughts, the ones with the greatest meaning.[7] Other scientists have maintained that biological factors alone explain dreams, that a dream is "nothing but reflex responses to sensory stimuli or nothing but the byproduct of cerebral disturbances resulting from chemical and hormonal somatic imbalances."[8]

Only one subject in the whole study dismissed her dream as meaningless. Roberta was a fifty-seven-year-old woman who dreamed of her mother five days after she died from heart failure at age sixty-nine.

> I dreamed it was the day of her funeral. It was cold and raining. We were at the cemetery but hadn't buried her yet. They had taken the casket out of the hearse and some men were carrying it to the grave plot. I was really anxious that she was going to get wet. It was a nightmare. I was looking for someone to tell my fears to, but found no one. In fact, I didn't recognize anyone who was there. I was crying and really upset. That was it. My mind told me not to pay attention to the dream. It's just a dream. They don't mean anything.

Roberta had volunteered to be interviewed about the dream, but then chose to close down and dismiss the possibility of a meaning. This interview was the only one like it. Almost all the other dreamers found meanings in their dreams.

Some psychologists, like Clyde Reid, wrote that dreams are part of the realm of the spirit and come from that place in us where God's Spirit is present.[9] This idea, that dreams are messages from God or messages from spirits of the dead, is very old and exists in the world's major religions. The Torah of the Jews, the Gospels of Christians, and the Qu'ran of Muslims all have expressions of the belief that some dreams come from God.[10]

Many dreams in this study raised this question, making the dreamers wonder if the dead used dreams to communicate with the living. Faith, a twenty-four-year-old woman, dreamed of her best friend's boyfriend who died of a congenital heart disease at the age of twenty-three.

> I was in a bar and he walked in and I waved to him but he ignored me. I went over and asked, "Don't you know how to say hello?" He just smiled sadly and told me it wasn't a good time. I asked him what he was talking about. He said, "I keep trying to go to Gina (his girlfriend) but I can't get through to her. It's like she doesn't dream anymore." After I woke up, I was confused. The dream made me wonder if the dead find us through our dreams and try to communicate with us in them.

The dream raised questions about life after death and the possibility of the dead communicating with the living. At the time of the interview, Faith hadn't decided what to believe.

Some dreamers were clear in their decision to reject a spiritual interpretation. An example comes from May, a fifty-one-year-old woman, whose mother died of a heart attack at age seventy-six.

> The dream took me back to my childhood times. I was at the beach with mom. She was much younger, but I was my present age. We played ball, walked the beach, and talked. She apologized for not always being there when I was growing up. She told me not to worry about her and that she would always be near even if I couldn't see her.
>
> The dream told me I loved her and enjoyed the time we had together, but I don't believe in the ability of the dead to communicate with the living. I am skeptical about the idea of spirits and ghosts.

This is an example of a choice dreamers have, that is, to choose to believe in the spiritual reality of the dream or to remain skeptical about it.

Understanding grief

In this book, grief refers to all the ways the subjects reacted to the death of a friend or relative. The reactions were physical, social, psychological, and spiritual. The death affected their emotions, their thoughts, their behavior, and their beliefs. These reactions lasted for different lengths of time. Many scholars have studied this process, looking for universal models. For example, the idea that a bereaved person must accomplish certain tasks appeared first in 1944.[11] More recently, others have described these tasks in different configurations.[12] Some researchers have challenged the idea that there is a universal standard process but, rather, maintain the patterns of grieving are culturally conditioned.[13]

All agree that grief is a process of adjusting to the death over a period of time, but there is no consensus in regard to the duration of grief, or how long grief should last. In this study of 1064 subjects, 364 had their dreams within the first two months. That is 34%. The dreams of 684 subjects occurred within the first year. That's 64%. The dream interviews suggest that, for most of this sample population, the most intense aspects of grief occurred within the first few months after the death and during the first year. Yet for more than 25% of the subjects, the dreams occurred after two years and as long as 44 years after the death. In this book, this span of time between the death and the dream is one of the key identifiers for each dream interview. The readers can see for themselves how this time span relates to the other factors, such as the relationship with the deceased and the cause of death.

What is the goal of the grieving process? Up until the 1980's, grief was primarily thought of as emotional responses, the goal being "letting go" the emotional bonds with the deceased. Since then other researchers and therapists recognize the need to be equally focused on cognitive responses, such as understanding how things have changed since the death and what the death means personally to each survivor. Thomas Attig, for example, proposed that grief is primarily thinking about our relationships with the deceased, modifying our hopes and beliefs.[14] Robert A. Neimeyer maintains "the central process of grief is searching for meaning."[15] Most of the dreamers in this study recognized the dreams to be related to the struggle in their waking lives of adjusting to the death. The interviews revealed that almost every dreamer had thoughts about the death and found the dream to be meaningful.

Grief is a whole complex of reactions and responses people have after a death. We know there are certain things that people in grief do, such as remember the deceased and have thoughts and feelings about the death, but there are different factors that influence the responses, such as age, gender, relationship, and cause of death. There just is no universal formula to plot the course or set the timing. On the one hand, there are some things in common; on the other hand, each person's grief is unique.

Dreams about the dead are expressions of the experience of death. They are manifestations of the expressive need of humans.[16] When the experience is personally powerful, there is a greater need to find a way to express it. Usually people think that words are the way to express their grief, but there are many other ways to express grief such as music and images. Dreams about the dead are spontaneous images of a person's grief.

The study of dreams about the dead

Others have made this connection between grief and dreams about the dead. John Bowlby understood them to be expressions of the desire to find and recover the deceased.[17] Deirdre Barrett categorized these dreams as advice and leave-taking dreams and identified dream themes, such as denial, guilt, and acceptance of death.[18] Patricia Garfield also categorized themes and images that appear in dreams about the dead.[19] The recent book by T. J. Wray and Ann Proce focuses on four categories of "grief dreams," i.e., message dreams, reassurance dreams, visitation dreams, and trauma dreams.[20]

This book is based on 1064 interviews. The subjects were self-selected. Students and their friends or family members who had dreams about dead friends or family members were invited to be interviewed. A dream was accepted when the respondent confirmed that he or she had a dream while asleep, recognized the person in the dream who had died, and remembered it clearly after waking. The subjects were asked a series of questions which were based on an article about using dreams in counseling, but they were edited and added to in order to uncover cognitive as well as affective responses.[21]

The research was guided by the writings of Robert A. Neimeyer and others who made the case that our ideas about life are socially and personally constructed. What is needed, he wrote, is a phenomenological approach in which (in the case of this research) the dreamers are invited to share what they believe the dreams mean. Only then, he maintains, can the unique, yet common, perspectives be explored. Before we reduce dreams to some psychological theory, we need to really listen to what the dreamers make of the dream.[22] This book presents more than one hundred and sixty edited dream interviews in which the dreamers recount their dreams and discuss their emotional and cognitive responses. These are glimpses of people in grief. It affords us a snapshot of a unique process that can go on for years.

Profile of the subjects

There were 224 males in the study and 840 females. The fact that I teach at a primarily women's college may explain why there were so many more women than men. Louis LaGrand, however, thinks men are more reluctant to share these kinds of personal experiences than women because cultural expectations of maleness conflict with the quality of these dreams.[23]

The ages of the subjects at the time of the interview ranged from eighteen to ninety-three. The average age was thirty-five.

There were 933 subjects who identified themselves as Christians. That is 87% of the sample. In that number, 540 were Catholics. This is due to the fact that the college is a Catholic college. The overall percentage of Christians in the study is in line with the number of people in the United States who identify themselves as Christian.[24] So most of the dreamers were raised with Christian beliefs, images, and rituals, and these, at least, partly influenced their dreams and the meanings they found in them.

Results of the study: The six elements of grief

The interviews revealed six elements of grief. All the dreams had more than one element. The dreams presented different combinations of these elements. There was no particular order in which the elements showed up in the interviews.

Remembering

The first was the memory element. Significant memories of the deceased were either contained in the dream or were triggered by the dream. Louis LaGrand and others maintain that a major task of the grieving process is establishing a new relationship with the deceased.[25] For many subjects, a remembered presence was the way to do this. This explains the custom of promising the dying, "I'll never forget you." It is a pledge that the relationship will continue in this new way.

Here's an example of a dream that triggered the memory element of grief. Adelaide was a sixty-two-year-old woman whose aunt died many years before of a stroke at the age of sixty-three. The dream occurred thirty-five years after she died.

> In the dream I was visiting my aunt with my eldest son who was six months old. Since my aunt had no grandchildren of her own, she enjoyed my baby enormously. In the dream, she crooned to him and sang gypsy lullabies in Russian.
>
> The dream reminded me of how she imbued me with the feeling that I could handle anything. I could feel her love and support in the dream. It was a warm and wonderful feeling. I recalled her simple advice for raising children. She told me that my children would be my best teachers. I should watch them when they play, when they eat, when they sleep. I should observe how they interact in different situations with different people. In other words, I should pay attention to them and take my cues from them. She believed that paying attention offered more than any book. Her advice guided me in raising my three sons. Until I had this dream, I never fully realized how deeply I felt her loss. I gained so much wisdom from her. She really understood the role of a mother. I remembered how on nearly every Sunday, the family always ate at her house where we talked, laughed, and enjoyed each other's company. I realized the days spent in her house were some of the happiest days of my childhood. She was such a force in my life. I needed this dream and the memories it brought with it. My eldest son had died and the dream and the memories it brought back gave me strength. I couldn't have her with me in reality so I brought her back in a dream.

For this dreamer, the memories made her aunt present again and brought healing powers for the grief she had after her son's death.

Imagining

The second element was the use of the imagination. For example, some dreamers imagined what it would have been like if the deceased were still alive. Some imagined how they might still be present, watching over the bereaved. Others imagined what it would have been like if the deceased came back to life. Here's an example.

Veronica was a nineteen-year-old woman who told of a dream she had of her father who died when he was fifty-four.

> The dream started off with me at my house. My brother and grandmother were there. My mother came home and she was very excited. She told us that she had found a way that could bring my father back to life and that my father was coming home. My brother and I were really happy. And then he arrived. In the dream, we were happy to see him, at first, but things got uncomfortable. He had my dead dog with him, but the dog wasn't dead but was different. Through the whole dream my father carried the dog and the dog would snarl at us like he was protecting my father. It was really strange because the dog had never been like that. My father was upset at a lot of the changes that had occurred. He was so mad at my brother about something that he didn't even want to talk to him. He was mad at me because I wasn't living at home and because he didn't like my boyfriend. He was mad at my mother because she was engaged to be married and because we were moving to a new house. He was mean and my mother complained to my grandmother, his mother. Grandma told us we should leave and she would talk to her son. My mother packed us in our old car and drove us to a strange place. Somehow he followed us. He was really angry and then started to cry. We were all upset and we all were crying. My mother told him that he had to leave but he didn't want to. Then he said that we weren't allowed to leave. The dream was really scary. I woke up crying hysterically when the dream was over. The dream made me imagine that if my father came home he'd be unhappy and that if he were watching over us, he'd be unhappy with what he saw. What surprised me was that he was so angry. He always had a bad temper, but never that bad. I've never seen anyone that angry before. The dream tells me that, like my father, I am disappointed with my brother for not carrying out my father's wishes and taking care of my mother. It tells me that if my father were alive he would be disappointed in me for not living at home with my mom to be there when she is sick. (She has diabetes.) He'd also disapproved of my mother's boyfriend. Maybe it means I disapprove of my mom's relationship and feel that my father would be hurt by it. Selling the house is like we are leaving him and that's the part about us not being allowed to leave. The significance of the dog being with him is that she really is. The car that we no longer have was in the dream because it was the car we had when he was alive. The whole dream about him coming home is because deep down there's a part of me that wishes he could come home, but there's another part that realizes it would never work out.

Through the dream, Veronica used her imagination to become more realistic and aware of the adjustments that were needed after the death of her father.

Feeling

The third element was the affective responses of the bereaved. These included expressions of negative and positive emotional connection to the deceased. There were fears about the dead, sadness and loneliness, anger and guilt, as well as happiness and peacefulness. Here's an example.

Richard was a sixty-four-year-old man who dreamed of his father after he died at the age of ninety-four.

> I was falling through the air and was very scared. It was as if I fell out of a plane. I looked around as I plunged toward the earth and suddenly saw a figure floating rapidly toward me. He was younger and much bigger than me. He smiled as he reached out and scooped me into his arms. It was my father.
>
> When I woke up, I felt so safe and happy. The dream reminded me of the time when I was a kid and was hit by a car. My father rushed out into the street and scooped me up out of harm's way. I realized how much I miss the feelings of security my father always gave me when I was with him.

The dream resurrected memories and good feelings as well as the sense of loss. The dream is a glimpse of his grief. He was still grieving his father, nine years after the death.

Thinking

The fourth element was the cognitive response of the bereaved, the thoughts that the dream stirred up in the mind of the dreamer. These included questions about what really happened, or how much the deceased suffered before dying. There were negative thoughts about the deceased, but also thoughts of gratitude and appreciation. There were also questions about life after death. And there were questions about the dreaming process itself.

Thoughts that followed dreams were sometimes painful, raising disturbing questions. Here's an example from Michael, a thirty-four-year-old man, whose best friend was killed in an accident at the age of twenty-one. He had the dream three weeks later.

> It was a reminiscent dream of how we used to hang out after school and how much fun we used to have. In the dream, I was actually there with him, hanging out after school on the football field bleachers. Suddenly he was gone. All our friends were there still fooling around and talking, but he was gone. Nobody noticed that he was gone except me. Everybody else was still carrying on, joking around.

When I woke up, I felt confused. It made me realize how someone could be here one day and gone the next. The dream made me angry, because it was like he was forgotten so fast. He disappeared and everyone carried on as if nothing had happened. I got depressed after the dream. I wondered what I'd have to do to be remembered. Would I have to die a tragic death? Who would remember me after I died? How would they remember me? That dream really affected me. It still does.

For most dreamers, like Michael, the dreams were powerful experiences that influenced them deeply.

Gaining insights

The fifth element consisted of personal insights that bubbled up from the dream. These included awareness of the uncertainty in life, greater self-knowledge, and more realistic views of the relationships. There were realizations of the need to let go of emotional dependency on the deceased. Some dreams revealed the dreamer's need to be more forgiving and let go of grudges. And there were insights into the dreaming process.

Ruth was a nineteen-year-old woman when she related her dream of a childhood friend who was stabbed to death when they were only eleven years old. She had the dream five years later.

In the dream my friend was floating around in my room. When I asked him what he wanted, he told me I should let it go. I asked him what he meant. He repeated what he said, "Just let it go. Okay?" He seemed so insistent that I said, "Okay," and with that he disappeared.

After thinking about the dream, I realized he was telling me he was all right and that I should let go of the grudges I had for those who killed him. I didn't realize how I was holding onto them until that dream. I have to tell you what a big relief it is to be able to talk about the dream this way, to let it out in the open. I have been afraid to let anyone know how I feel. I never told anyone about the dream.

A powerful dream, like Ruth's, leaves the dreamer with a need to tell someone about it. But the interviews revealed it was common for dreamers to be fearful of negative reactions. They feared listeners would devalue something they thought was special.

Personal insights often focused on the relationship with the deceased. Dreams commonly reminded the dreamers of things about the relationship. These memories led to greater awareness of the value of the relationship. Judith, a forty-five-year-old woman, dreamed of her ex-mother-in-law four years after she died from cancer.

> In the dream I was back living in the apartment under her apartment. I heard pounding, like hammering, so I climbed the stairs and opened the door and saw her cutting up meat to makes pastels. She invited me to join her for a cup of coffee. It was so real.
>
> When I woke up I felt very happy. The dream reminded me how she took time to teach me how to cook. It made me realize that she loved me not just because I was married to her son but for me. At the time of the dream, I wasn't talking to my own mother and I needed to know that someone loved me who was a mother to me, and she did.

Believing

The sixth element was spiritual. This consisted of beliefs about life and death. For example, some believed that the dreams were visits from the dead, often offering a chance to say goodbye or resolve conflicts. Others believed that the dreams were messages from the dead; these messages included advice, warnings, requests, and apologies. Finally, some believed that the dreams contained true images of or information about the afterlife.

One belief that was common in the dream interviews was that the relationship with the deceased continued. Shameeka was twenty-four years old when she related how she dreamed of her uncle two months after he died at the age of seventy-two.

> In the dream I saw my uncle pull his truck into our driveway. I felt excited like I had for years as a kid whenever I would see his truck. It meant I would get a quarter and some candy. I ran to him and he hugged me, then he looked in my ear and chirped like a bird. He always did this and would say that as long as there was a little chick living in my ear then I was still his little birdie. Then he gave me a quarter and some candy, got back in his truck, and drove off but not before I told him that I loved him and he said he would always love his little birdie.
>
> Then I woke up smiling. The dream made me remember all the times he did this. Every week he would do this little ritual, chirp in my ear and give me a quarter and some candy. Looking back, I remembered I used to love that chirp. After he died, I was worried he might not know how much he meant to me. The dream made me believe that he knows because he is listening right now, for I am still his little birdie. Although I do not have the sensitivity to hear it, I know he chirps for me when I need him. The dream reassured me that no matter how old I get, he will always see that little chick inside my ear. It is as though no matter how unbearable life may seem, he is still there to support his little birdie.

It was the uncle's ritual expression of his affection that makes this dream so powerful.

Some dreams contained images of the afterlife. Sometimes these images confused the dreamers. Bessie was sixty years old when she told how her father died from a brain tumor at age sixty-two. The next day she dreamed of him. She still remembered it very clearly after many years.

> In the dream, I saw my father ascending a long staircase. I called to him to come back, but he told me his life on earth was finished. At the top of the stairs, there was a door. When he reached the door, he knocked on it. His long-since-dead sister opened the door and welcomed him. Before he passed through the doorway, he turned toward me and told me not to cry. He said he was no longer in pain. He told me to tell mom not to cry but to continue on with life as if he were still around. Then he described the place he was entering as very peaceful and cheerful. He said he would be in the company of deceased relatives and friends who had been waiting for him to arrive. He told me that some day we would all be together again. Finally, he waved to me and followed his sister into the light. When the door closed, I woke up.
>
> The dream confused me. It made me question whether heaven exists as I've been taught in church or if it is the way the dream had it. The dream was very real. I still don't know.

Vivid dreams like this often lead to questions about what the dreamer had previously been taught to believe about life after death.

Organization of the study

All of the dreams in this study had more than one element. The elements came in various clusters. That is why it would be misleading and confusing to organize the book using these elements as a framework. Instead it seemed better to use the natural categories of the different relationships between the deceased and the dreamer. Within each of these relationship categories, the reader will be able to see how different clusters of these elements present themselves.

The interviews revealed the importance of these relationships. I agree with Nancy Moos who maintained that family dynamics, that is, relationships are more important than stages or tasks of grieving.[26] Therefore, the chapters are arranged according to relationships. There are chapters on dreams about grandparents, mothers, fathers, brothers, sisters, and cousins, wives and husbands, sons and daughters, and friends. I've also chosen this order to make it easier for readers to find dreams similar to the ones they're interested in.

Chapter 2: Dreams about Grandparents

There were 233 dreams about grandparents in the study. Grandparents and grandchildren can form a connection that is free of the responsibilities, duties, and inevitable conflicts that characterize parent-child relationships. They connect their grandchildren to the values and perspectives of an earlier generation. Although the dream experiences of dead grandparents varied widely, what was clear in most interviews was the important part grandparents played in the dreamers' lives.

Life is short

In the first example, Anne, a twenty-two-year-old woman dreamed of her grandfather one year after he died of a heart attack at the age of sixty-seven.

> I was sitting in the living room of his house talking to him about school and stuff. Suddenly he was gone. I called to grandma who was in the kitchen and asked her where grandpa had gone, but she didn't answer. That's when I woke up.
> I was confused about why he left in the middle of the conversation. I felt sad and realized how much I missed him. I used to visit all the time. I loved to talk with him about school and boys and stuff. I missed him more than I realized. The dream reminded me that life is short; someone can die in the middle of a conversation. The dream taught me to appreciate people while they are still around and not take them for granted.

Anne found the dream meaningful in two ways. First, it made her realize the relative shortness of life. While most of the deaths in this relationship were natural and expected (189), 44 were unexpected like Anne's grandfather's heart attack. So she is affected differently because of the way he died. Secondly, the dream made her more aware of the extent of her own sadness, and how much her grandfather had cared for her, and how much she missed that. One hundred and thirty-five dreamers who dreamed of grandparents said the dream made them realize how much their grandparent loved them. That was 57% of this group.

Unresolved issues

Many dreams reminded the dreamers of unresolved issues in the relationship that were eating away inside them. Barbara, a twenty-three-year-old, told of a dream she had four months after her ninety-eight-year-old grandfather died.

> He was on his deathbed and calling out to me. It was very foggy and I couldn't tell where I was. I tried to reach him but I never quite got to him. He got angry and started yelling at me for breaking my promise to be there for him and I started crying. Eventually his voice became fainter until I couldn't hear him any more. It seemed like he got farther and farther away until he was gone.
>
> After the dream, I felt guilty about not being there when he died, but I also was angry at my mother who decided not to take me with her to see him when he was near death. He was in a nursing home more than two hours away. The dream made me realize that I want to be close to my family and not end up so far away like him. After the dream, I went to church and prayed for him and to him and made my peace with him. Then my anger toward my mother lessened and the dream stopped reoccurring.

The dream helped Barbara identify her guilt at not keeping her promise to her grandfather and her anger at her mother. Through prayer, she was able to resolve these two unfinished parts of her grief. This is one example of the kind of rituals that are inherited through our families.

Regrets

Regrets are a common theme in dreams about the dead. Out of 1064 dreams, 388 of the dreamers said the dreams uncovered regrets they had about the relationship; that is 36.5%. Among the dreams of grandparents, 89 (38%) expressed regrets about the relationship. Here's an example. Three months after her eighty-five-year-old grandmother died of pneumonia, Charlene, a forty-seven-year-old woman, said she had this dream for the first time. She had it several times after that.

> Everything was dark. I could hear her calling me but I had no voice to answer her. She sounded a little afraid and I kept trying to answer her but I didn't have any voice. She knew I was there because she asked a question and

was waiting for my answer, so patiently, like when I was little. She didn't even get upset that I was not answering her. I started to cry because I was trying to tell her something but couldn't.

When I woke up, I felt bad that I hadn't called her on the phone more often. I regretted being too busy to call. The dream reminded me of how when I was little, I'd visit her for the weekend. She'd take me shopping or we would go to the movies or bake things to eat I wouldn't get at home. After the dream, I felt very guilty that I didn't call her more often, especially when she was sick. In the dream, I was trying to help her because I wasn't there when she died. I am very sorry for that. No one ever asks me about her anymore and if I bring her up, they change the subject because they think I'm going to cry.

The dream showed Charlene that she still has tears inside over her grandmother. She still had a need to reminisce about her and express both her appreciation and her regrets. Unfortunately, she had difficulty finding a good listener, someone who could understand her grief.

Negative aspects of one's familial inheritance

We all inherit a host of attitudes and values from our family. For some it could be the value of hard work; for others it might be the value of education. In the next dream, the dreamer discovered aspects of her inheritance that she had not realized before.

Denise, a thirty-six-year-old woman, related her dream about her great-grandmother which occurred twenty years after her death.

I had the dream recently. In the dream, my family and I were as we were back in time. I think we were in Brooklyn where my mother was raised by her mother and grandmother. In the dream, my mother and I were the same age which was strange. My great-grandmother was there in the background cooking. My mother was trying to explain to me how my great-grandmother raised her wrong and that was why she turned out the way she did. For example, she told me her grandmother never pushed her to go to school. The dream was mostly this conversation with my mother.

I remember waking up and feeling heavy, knowing I really wanted to remember the dream; it was very powerful. I felt bad because it was about how things went wrong in our family. I felt upset because it also affected me. By my mother telling me how things went wrong, she was also trying to explain to me what went wrong in raising me. So I was upset for me and her. I was also upset because I put my great-grandmother on a pedestal and I didn't want to hear anything negative about her. It made me think why things are the way they are in my family, why my mother is the way she is, and what happened to her. In the dream, my mother was telling me how she didn't take her life seriously and I realized how I feel about myself has a lot to do with how they felt about themselves. The dream is all about females. It was my brother who was expected to take his life seriously and choose a career. The basic values in our family haven't changed over the generations. I am expected to get married, as was my grandmother and mother. My mother didn't have the opportunity to do what she wanted to do and was frustrated. The conflicts I experience in my life today are expressed in the dream. Now I understand why it is so difficult for me to make decisions, to take my life seriously. My great-grandmother affected my grandmother, my mother, and me. I woke up feeling like crying, like mourning the whole thing. The dream was about regrets over what didn't happen, what my great grandmother didn't do to help my mother and what my mother didn't do to overcome them. The dream made me think of my life, and what this all means in terms of me as a woman. The dream pointed to something I could do; I could have a conversation with my mother about all this. I realized I usually avoid talking with my mom about stuff like this. The dream offered me an opportunity to have a new relationship with my mother in terms of what we've inherited. It really was a powerful dream.

This is an insightful dream offering Denise a new way of understanding herself and her family, back three generations. Not everything about our family is positive. Over all, only 127 dreamers (11.9%) said the dream reminded them of something negative about the deceased, but among the dreams about grandparents, 18 dreamers (14%) said so. Denise's dream is an example. The dream also suggested something she could do about it, that is, talk to her mother about the dream and its meaning.

Positive aspects of one's familial inheritance

In the following dream, Evelyn, a forty-one-year-old woman, came to appreciate something she inherited from her grandfather who died at the age of eighty-two. She dreamed of him twenty years later.

> I was a child again back in the neighborhood where I grew up. My sister, my cousin, and I were in grandpa's big yellow Cadillac and he was taking us to the candy store. (This really happened when we were young.) He took us in and told us to pick out one candy bar each. We were all laughing and having a great time. We all climbed into the back seat and began to eat our candy bars as he drove us home. Then I woke up.
> The dream made me feel warm and happy. The dream reminded me of the good times I had with him and how he always took us once a week when we were young to get a candy bar of our choice. I realized that I did the same thing for my kids and that I must have gotten the idea from him. It made me aware of how important rituals like this are in families.

The dream helped Evelyn see that inherited family rituals are ways members of families express love for each other. They spare us from having to create new rituals and they join consecutive generations with memorable bonds of affection.

The next dream also led the dreamer to appreciate a grandparent. Frances, a thirty-six-year-old, told of her dream about her grandmother who died eight years earlier of a brain hemorrhage at the age of sixty-eight.

> I was in her house, sitting at the kitchen table with her. We were just talking and preparing supper for when grandpa came home from work. I woke up before he came home. The dream made me feel very sad. I longed for the times in my childhood that I spent with them. They were such stable people. I thought of how I took those moments for granted. I remembered spending many, many days doing average things with my grandmother — sewing, cooking, even hanging laundry with her in the back yard. She was happy and so was I. She found satisfaction in doing these things. They weren't chores; they were fun.
>
> Before the dream, I never realized how precious those times spent with her were. At the time of the dream, I was newly married, so I think the dream about being back in my grandmother's home gave me a great sense of stability and helped me cope with all the changes going on in my life. This interview has awakened in me a new depth of appreciation for my grandmother.

Through the dream, Frances recalled meaningful memories that led to her insight. She realized her inner attitude toward what she did determined whether she was happy or not. Frances was feeling peer pressure to view certain activities in married life as burdensome. The dream reminded her of her grandmother and revealed the secret of being happy.

Healing dreams

Memories, recalled in a dream, can not only enlighten but also heal. Adam, a thirty-year-old man, dreamed of his grandmother five years after she died at eighty-three.

> The dream presented a real memory of my family. We were all going to my grandmother's house to visit. I distinctly remembered the smell of the house and the ambience of that particular environment. My grandmother was German and always cooked different kinds of German dishes. The house smelled fruity from the apple and cherry pies she was baking. She made the most delicious chocolate pudding with the best homemade whipped cream on top. This dream was a typical visit where we sat around the dining room table talking and laughing while getting ready to eat. I woke up feeling disappointed that I did not have a chance to eat dinner. I wanted the dream to continue. It made me feel warm and safe. I woke up wishing I still could have those wonderful experiences with her.
>
> The dream made me realize the good times I shared with my grandmother were because she was generous, full of life, and had an incredible sense of humor. I wish she were still around not only to share such precious moments, but also to meet special people that I currently have in my life. When I had the

dream, I was under a lot of stress at work and felt very insecure. Somehow the dream allowed me to put myself in a safe environment where I experienced freedom from any kind of stress and pressure. It gave me an emotional break from my inner turmoil. It reminded me of the importance of keeping close family ties and appreciating my elders. As a result of the dream, I try to connect with older members of my family in special ways because they will not be around forever.

The dream gave Adam an emotional break from the stress of his work environment as well as the insight that family is far more important than work.

Gladys was a twenty-three-year-old woman who dreamed of her grandmother three years after she died at age seventy-eight.

In the dream, I was in her home and it was morning. She came downstairs to the kitchen, sat down, and started to knit. I sat down and in front of me on the table was a glass of milk and a bowl of hot oatmeal which had been my favorite breakfast as a child. I asked her what she was making and she said she was making me an afghan so I wouldn't get cold at night. I hugged her and told her I loved her and I was sorry I didn't visit her more often. She brushed it off and she told me it was okay, that she understood.

The dream reminded me of how we drifted apart the last few years before her death. I also thought about how forgiving and caring my grandmother was and how I should be that way too. I realized everyone makes mistakes like this and I shouldn't beat myself up or make myself feel miserable for it but forgive myself. The dream made me feel very relieved and loved. It showed me how important it is to stay close to the people we love and not take them for granted. I have been very busy with college and work and I don't get to see my mother or family much. I'm afraid I will regret this later on in life and have resolved to see them more often.

This dream offered Gladys a chance to see her life from a different perspective. This new view of things led her to want to change her priorities. She also came to appreciate her grandmother's good example of a caring and forgiving woman.

Henrietta's dream is also a good example of the imaginative element. Her dream was about a dragon and her grandfather. She was twenty years old when she told about her dream which she had three years after he died at the age of seventy-five.

In the dream, I was about three years old. He was holding me on his lap while we sat looking out the window. I was wearing my pajamas and he was wearing his work clothes. It was starting to get dark; the sun had set and the clouds were purple. It was a really comforting atmosphere. He was talking to me when a dragon came around from behind the house. My grandfather pointed towards the dragon and told me that it wouldn't hurt us. The dragon was as big as the house. The dragon slowly came up to the window, but he didn't dart at us. Then he slowly stomped away. The dragon was dark green with big purple scales. The dragon simply walked away. My grandfather kept quietly talking to me. The trees were swaying and the dream ended.

The dream reminded me that my grandfather used to tuck me in at bedtime and would tell me stories. When I was little, I loved listening to "Puff the Magic Dragon." My grandfather loved animals and would never hurt one. The dream reminded me that whenever I was with him, I felt safe and secure. He never raised his voice at me. Remembering this dream makes me feel relaxed. When I was young, I thought he was pretty neat. Now, I think about him as being one the coolest people I have ever known. At the time of the dream, my parents were getting divorced. It was really scary for me and the dream just made the situation easier to handle. It told me not to be afraid of things, no matter how big they seem. Something as big as a dragon could have hurt us, but it didn't. Nothing is really as bad as it seems.

I was taught that when you dream of the dead, the deceased is trying to communicate with you, to remind you not to forget about them, so I went to church and lit a candle in his memory. At other times, after I dreamed of him, I visited his grave and brought flowers. I was brought up that way. Anyway, he was the best.

Most of the dreamers were taught how to think about dreams of the dead and how to respond to them. Henrietta inherited specific instructions from her mother when she was young.

Dreams often contain or invoke healing memories. Bruce was fifty-one when he related the dream he had of his grandfather who died at the age of seventy-nine, some forty years earlier.

I dreamt that I was a small boy at my grandparent's apartment in New York. It was summertime. They lived on the fourth floor and I was out on the fire escape looking at the parade as it passed by the Catholic Church across the street. It was a feast day. My grandfather was the leader of the parade, because he was the president of the Knights of Columbus. We called him "Big Grandpa." All of a sudden he came up behind me and put his arms around me. He had brought me some provolone cheese and asked me, "Do you like the music?" Then, he was gone and I woke up.

It was good to have been there, reliving a happy time. I felt like I really belonged. It reinforced the importance of family. It made me remember that the simple things are beautiful and valuable. It got me thinking how my dad is getting old and I realize that I won't have him around much longer. Only he and my uncle are left. There were four other brothers who have already died. Big Grandpa was the bedrock. He always said, "Hold your head up high. Always do what is right. If you look in the mirror and like what you see, no one can take that away from you." I have recently lost my job. Although I try to hide it, I was fired. I don't like myself and what I have become, a dual personality. The dream made me realize how grateful I should be. I am very lucky. I really am loved. I really mean it. I am grateful for my family and my children. I regret buying into the system which has made me sick, living a double life. I have tried hard not to let my family down, but I lost myself along the way. My father's health and memory are failing. The dream gave me a second chance. It's like medicine I needed to get well.

The dream triggered a series of powerful memories about his grandfather and family as well as a life review. It helped Bruce gain a fresh perspective on how he wanted to lead his life and the changes he needed to make.

Is there life after death?

Carl was a nineteen-year-old male who dreamed of his grandmother three months after she died at age eighty.

> In the dream, I was walking by her room and looked in and saw an apparition of her. She looked very natural and real yet like a ghost. I knew she was dead and just stood there staring at her. She didn't seem to see me. I woke up in a cold sweat. The dream was so real. It opened up a lot of questions, like when someone dies, what happens to her soul? When someone dies, her body falls to the floor and stays there until someone moves it, but what I saw was so real even though it was a dream, it made me wonder. I still wonder. You are the only one I've ever told the dream to. It still scares me.

Among those who dreamed of grandparents, 97 (41%) said the dream made them think about their beliefs about life after death. Carl was one example. He was raised in a non-religious family in which discussions about beliefs in life after death never occurred. He had no inherited family beliefs or rituals to fall back on. The idea of a soul came from school and popular culture. The dream confronted Carl with the possibility of realities he had never seriously addressed. It challenged his view of things and left him uncertain and "scared."

A change of belief

The next dream changed the dreamer's faith in an afterlife and her attitude toward people who turn to religion in the face of death. Irene was a nineteen-year-old woman whose grandmother died shortly after a series of strokes. She was sixty-four. She died one month before the dream.

> It was dark. She appeared dressed in white. There was a light behind her but I could see her face. She looked just like before the stroke. She just stood and smiled at me then faded away. I waved and said goodbye.
> I felt so good to see her that way. When she died, I felt hate towards God and everything like that. She showed up in the dream and it changed everything. She made me believe. The dream told me there is something after death so I shouldn't hate what happened. Now I believe she is always there for me,

that she is always going to be around. I believe I can talk to her if I want. She is still in my life no matter where she is, but I also believe she is somewhere safe. The dream felt so real, like she was standing right here. I really felt her.

It made me think about how my mother and aunt handled her death. Right away they went to church and everything like that and it seemed to help them. I still don't go but now I understand why they go, how they feel. That's their sanctuary; they go to church so they can get more with God and those who have died, and I don't put that down anymore.

Irene's dream is a good example of how a dream can lead to a changed perspective about things. In this case, Irene became more open and respectful of the religious traditions of others.

Did I do the right thing?

In the following dream, Dan, a twenty-one-year-old man, not only found confirmation of life after death, but also revisited some unanswered questions about his grandfather's death. Dan had the dream three months after his grandfather died of insulin shock.

I had a friend with me and we were at a summer barbeque; we always had barbeques at my house and there were always lots of family. I loved the barbeques. So I brought my friend around and was introducing him to everybody, all my aunts, uncles, and cousins. We walked through the car port meeting everybody, and we got to the backyard and met more people. There was a redwood picnic table in the backyard with an umbrella and my grandfather was sitting by it. He held his cane and had on a blue fisherman's hat. I had my back to him and hadn't seen him, so he said to me, "Hey, boy, you're not going to introduce me?" I turned around and I looked and it was him right there leaning on his cane and looking at me. I was definitely scared at first. I looked into his eyes and was surprised. They were clear and I could see that he could see me. (Because of diabetes, he was blind before he died and his eyes had been cloudy.) He said "It's me. Don't be scared." Then my grandfather told me that I should have given him some brownies at the hospital when he was alive. (I used to make brownies for him.) The hospital had given him too much insulin; that is what put him into shock. When I went to see him at the hospital, I brought the brownies for him and I wanted to give them to him, but my mother said I couldn't give them to him in his condition. Maybe if I had given him the brownies there would have been a different outcome. So he was saying that I should have given him the brownies. I had felt guilty about not giving him the brownies. I had sat in the car for hours the day he died, going over and over in my mind, "What if I had given him the brownies?" At that point in the dream I said to him, "Wait a second; let me get mom." I was trying to call my mother; I was yelling but nobody heard me.

When I did wake up I was crying and upset. I never had a dream like this before. I told my mother about the dream and we talked for a long time because

I was scared, yet I felt happy, happy to have seen him, also happy to know that there is a higher power. It made me think about the afterlife. It made me believe that there is one. For me, it answered the question what happens when you die. Now I believe you are taken into God's hands as it says in the Bible. The dream gave me peace of mind. I felt that he told me that I should have followed my heart. I never realized that the dream affected me so much until I did this interview.

Among those who dreamed of grandparents, 103 subjects (44%) said they, like Dan, were comforted by the dream.

Not so heavenly

Joanne, a twenty-nine-year-old woman, spoke of her dream about her grandmother who died of cancer. Joanne had the dream eight years after the death.

> In the dream, my friend ran into my room and screamed that my grandmother was coming, and then ran away. The door started to open and I kept telling myself that she was dead and couldn't come back. I covered my eyes with my hands but peeked under them and saw her feet. Gradually, I saw her completely. She looked the same except tired and sad. She said she came back to see me because she knew my mother and I were worried about my sister's health. She told me not to worry, that my sister would be fine. I felt comfortable enough to ask her if she was happy where she was. She sadly said she wasn't. When I asked her why not, she answered, "At night I am frightened when the torments start." At that I tried to give her a hug but she vanished.
>
> I felt really bad for her and helpless. There was nothing I could do to take away her pain. I also felt a little guilty because I belonged to a different religion than she did and wondered if this is why she was suffering.

The negative state of her grandmother overshadowed the comforting message Joanne's grandmother brought her about her sister. Joanne had been raised in a church where she was taught that only those who belonged to that church would be spiritually saved. She had not believed this, but the dream raised questions, leaving her confused. Among those who dreamed of grandparents, 89 subjects (38%) said the dream left them confused because something in the dream was out of sync with what they had learned.

Final goodbye

Janelle, a twenty-two-year-old woman, related a dream she had when she was fifteen, two days after her sixty-five-year-old grandfather died suddenly of a heart attack.

I went to visit grandma. Grandpa was sitting in his favorite chair on the front porch, drinking a beer and smoking his pipe like he always did. He called me over so he could give me a hug. I was afraid and started to cry because I knew he was dead. He said to me, "You don't have to fear the dead; it's only the living you need to fear." He asked again for me to come over because I wouldn't get another chance to say goodbye, so I went to him and he gave me a hug and a kiss on the forehead. It was so real. I can remember the smell of his pipe tobacco in the dream.

When I woke up, it really hit me that I would never see him again. My cousin and I had the same dream; we were his favorites and this dream confirmed it for us. The dream gave me a sense of closure because I had a chance to say goodbye.

Too often, the complexity of our lives prevents us from saying goodbye before a loved one dies, but saying goodbye should be seen as a priority. The Torah of the Jewish people says that this is one of God's 613 commandments. To skip the opportunity to say goodbye would hang over the head of the bereaved like a dark cloud. The dream gave Janelle a second chance to complete the relationship and attain peace. Janelle was one of 89 dreamers of grand-parents (36.5%) who said the dream made them feel peaceful.

I've been watching you

Karen was twenty-one and had the dream ten years after her grandfather died at the age of seventy-two.

I was walking along the paths of a park by the shore. When I was a child, he would take me there. I got to the large stone structure and I saw a man sitting there. He was very quiet and dressed in knickers, a style popular in the 1930's. I took a closer look and realized it was him but he was much younger, about my age. (I have a picture of him looking like this that my mom gave me.) I looked at my hands and they were all wrinkled and old looking. I sat down and said hello and asked if he knew who I was. He said that he did and then asked me how I've been. We started talking. He sounded like he'd been watching me for the last ten years. He knew everything that had been going on in my life. It was really weird. He started remembering funny episodes from the past. I asked him if he could see something about my future and he said that everything was going to be okay.

I woke up in a cold sweat. I looked at my hands and they were normal, but I was shaking. I just had a conversation with a man who'd been dead for ten years. As a child, I always looked up to him. We were very close and he was always my support, for example, when my mother yelled at me. I guess I was looking for support at that time although I don't remember thinking of him. I guess I needed his reassurance and he gave it to me.

Among those who dreamed of grandparents, 132 (56.7%) said they under-stood the dream to mean that the grandparents were watching over their grand-children. This came as a surprise to many, like Karen.

A promised visit

The next dream is different from Karen's. Two months after Linda's grand-mother died, she had this dream. Linda was twenty-two at the time.

> In the dream, I woke up feeling very groggy. I walked into the bathroom. When I looked into the mirror, I noticed vapor rising out of the toilet bowl. The vapor turned into an image of my grandmother. She wasn't solid, but was sort of thick fog. I began to ask her questions such as how she was and what it was like and what happened after she died. In response she told me that it is amazing and beautiful in heaven—more than she ever believed it could be. She also said that she had promised me that she would come back and that is why she was here. I told her that I really missed her. She said that she would see me some day and that she loved me very much. The next thing I knew, my grandmother was transformed back into vapor and vanished into the toilet bowl.
>
> The dream left me feeling very content knowing that she remembered to come back to let me know that there is life after death. I was relieved and not scared. It brought back memories of when I was five years old. I was worried about death, in particular her death, because she was the oldest in the family and, I thought the next one to die. So I asked her to come back after she died to tell me how it was. The dream reminded me of my worries and desire for answers about life after death. She didn't forget.

No need to fear death

There are details about life after death in the next dream. Maria, a nineteen-year-old, dreamed of her seventy-four-year-old grandmother two months after she died of heart failure at home in her sleep.

> The dream began with me going to my Grandmother's apartment to clean it out at the request of the landlord. While outside the apartment, I was startled to see my Grandmother's kitchen light on. No one had been in it for a month and I thought that it wasn't good that the light had been left on all that time, so I hurried up. In the hallway, outside the apartment, I smelled someone making coffee. The door to her apartment opened straight into the kitchen and when I entered I saw my grandmother sitting at the table with three cups of coffee. She gave me a big smile like she was expecting me. I screamed, "You're alive," and hugged her and began to cry. Then I said, "But you're dead." She responded with a laugh. Then I told her my aunt was coming and she said, "I know." Then I noticed the three cups of coffee on the table. I told her we couldn't find her

ring and asked her where she kept it. She said that she had it and stretched out her hand and showed it to me. I asked, "How did you take it with you?" And she just smiled and shrugged her shoulders. Just then the doorbell rang and it was my aunt. I met her at the door and said I had a surprise for her. She thought I had found the ring but I told her it was better than that. I made her close her eyes and led her into the kitchen. When she opened her eyes and saw her mother she screamed and fell into her arms. After the tearful reunion, we sat at the table and discussed the night she died. She said, "After you all had gone home, I went to the commode and got back into bed, closed my eyes and I was there." Then she smiled and was quiet. I began to cry when I heard my aunt say to her mother, "Mommy, tell me about it." Grandmother stared off in the distance then closed her eyes and took a deep breath, "It's more beautiful than you can imagine." When she opened her eyes I looked into them and asked, "Did you see Him? Did you see Jesus?" A big smile appeared on her face and big tears rolled down her cheeks. Then we all hugged each other for a long time shedding tears of joy.

Then suddenly we were in the dining room and the whole family was sitting at the table and grandma was at the head. Everyone was eating and laughing. Grandmother quietly watched, enjoying the happy scene. Then she stood up and everyone became quiet and looked at her. She began to get hazy but her face remained clearly visible. She made eye contact with each family member. I began to cry because I knew she was getting ready to leave. "I love each and every one of you. Always remember, you are a family. No matter what, you are a family." She then faded away and I woke up crying.

The dream left me with a great feeling of happiness and peace especially when she told me that after going to bed she closed her eyes and when she opened them again she was "there" or in heaven. I no longer fear death.

Maria said the primary meaning of the dream was confirmation of her inherited beliefs about life after death. The message about family, delivered by grandma in the dream, was not the point. The existence of heaven was.

Message: Have the baby

Other dreams were understood to be primarily messages from the dead. In the following dream Nancy was a forty-two-year-old woman who dreamed of her grandfather five years after he died at the age of eighty-six.

At the time of the dream I was pregnant. I was in the process of having to make a decision whether to abort the baby or risk my life to bring the baby to term. I dreamed that he was sitting at my bedside. He placed his hand on my stomach and told me to stop crying. He also told me not to worry because the baby was going to be all right and that I should not abort the baby.

The dream made me happy and sad at the same time. I missed him so much and longed to talk to him. His love reminded me of the perfect love God has for his children. My grandfather was special; I could have told him my darkest secret and would have felt safe. I realized how his love made me feel good about myself. The sad part was that I couldn't continue the conversation with him, but I felt he had given me the answer to my prayers. I was not surprised by the dream. I believed that he was always watching over me. At the time of the dream, I was going through a rough emotional time. I had almost lost my life during my first pregnancy. I lost the baby and was told that I was not to get pregnant again, but I did. The doctors were telling me I had to terminate the pregnancy and my husband was really worried for my health, but somewhere deep down inside I knew that I would be okay. The dream confirmed my belief that death doesn't sever the relationship we have with our dead loved ones. It answered my question about whether I was risking my life to have the baby. My husband had never met my grandfather, but he had heard me talk about him constantly, so, after I told him the dream, without a second thought, he supported my decision to have the baby. My doctors and my family thought that I was crazy; they even questioned my sanity. But when I told my mother about the dream, she smiled and said to me, "God is with you." My son is now 15 years old and I am the mother of two boys.

Message: Take on a new role in the family

When someone in a family dies, social adjustments need to be made. Survivors need to step up and take over the roles filled by the deceased. This process is expressed in the following dream in which the dead grandfather conferred on his grandson a new role in the family. Emory was thirty-two years old when he dreamed of his grandfather one year after he died at the age of eighty-four.

I was standing out back on a summer evening, cleaning up the barbeque. Suddenly my grandfather walked up to me. I was scared because I knew he was dead, but also because he looked angry. He didn't say hello or anything but started talking about one of my cousins and how he was really upset about how she was acting. Then he told me that he couldn't do it anymore, so he wanted me to talk to her and straighten her out. I protested but he was insistent. Only after I promised I would talk to her did he smile, pat me on the shoulder and say, "That's my boy." Then he turned and walked away.

The dream left me really confused and bothered. I was wondering what my cousin had done to get him so worked up. It turned out she was fighting with two other relatives. I was really bothered that he came to me with the problem and dumped it in my lap. The dream told me that I should act as mediator for problems in my family, but I still don't know why it should be me!

Emory didn't get a message of comfort. The message in his dream challenged him. He was still resistant to his new role in the family at the time of the interview.

Message: Visit the grave and pray

Many young people inherit from their families, customs, like visiting cemeteries and offering prayers for the dead. Sometimes these rituals are neglected. In the next dream, the dead grandfather asked that they be continued. Olivia was a twenty-two-year-old woman who dreamed of her grandfather two years after he died of cancer at the age of seventy-nine.

> I was sitting in the living room by myself reading a magazine. Suddenly he appeared standing by the door. He looked a little annoyed. He looked around as if to see if anyone else was around and then asked me why no one visited him in the cemetery. He also said, "It would be nice if you brought some flowers." Then he told me to tell grandma to pray more often to him and he would protect her. I promised to tell the others and to personally go and visit him. He smiled and said, "Good." Then he turned and left.
>
> The dream was so real. A few days before I had the dream, I had told my family that we ought to visit him in the cemetery since it had been a while. The dream made me confident that he was doing fine and that there really is life after death. I imagined he must miss the family. I miss him a lot and wish he was still here. By going to his grave, I knew I would feel closer to him and hoped he would feel less lonely. I went the next day and try to go once a month.

Rituals of remembrance are certainly good for survivors in helping them through the grief process. Olivia's dream told her that they were important for the deceased as well.[27]

Chapter 3: Dreams about Mothers

Parents, usually, have the greatest influence on what their children become. It is their example that informs them how to be male or female, husbands or wives, mothers or fathers. They are the primary responders to children's needs. The responsibilities of parenting are many; traditionally most of them are thought to belong to mothers. Among the 1064 dreams, 156 of the dreams (14.7%) were about mothers who had died. No one is a faultless parent, because parents have inherited parenting models that were inevitably flawed. When a parent dies, the surviving son or daughter begins a long grieving process. In this chapter and the next, the dreams offer glimpses of the challenges of grief faced by the dreamers.

She is really gone

Fully accepting the death of a parent and adjusting to the absence of their emotional support is part of grief. Pauline was twenty-three when she related this dream about her mother who died at the age of forty-six.

> I dreamed I saw her standing outside a park. When I first looked at her, she was fine, but the closer I got the worse she looked. She didn't look like a corpse but a decaying body. I recognized her and went to hug her because I was so happy to see her, but when I touched her, she just fell apart.
>
> The dream left me feeling frightened, sad, and confused. This is what I thought the dream meant. My mom had been suffering from lung cancer and that's why she was falling apart. Her decaying body also represented my mental state. I was falling apart. The dream was like a wake-up call. It made me realize she is really gone. It made me think about why I was still trying to hold onto her. The shocking image was meant to get me to fully accept the reality that my mother is no longer around to give me hugs and satisfy my other needs.

In a good relationship, like between Pauline and her mother, the grief can last for years. In this case, the dream occurred four years after the death. It was a benchmark in her grieving process. There is no universal timetable for grief. Each grief is unique. Among the subjects who dreamed of their mothers, like Pauline, 55 (35%) said the dream made them realize their mothers were really dead.

The next dream also helped the dreamer to accept the finality of his mother's death but offered much more besides. Frank was a nineteen-year-old man whose mother died from a cerebral hemorrhage at the age of forty-six. She was in a coma for a few weeks before she died. He had the dream a few months later.

> In the dream, I woke up one morning and walked down the stairs of my house and entered the kitchen. I found my mom there preparing breakfast for me, like she used to. The dream seemed so real that I could smell the bacon. My mouth was watering. I was shocked that she was so full of life and yet I knew she was dead. After we ate I walked towards the front door to leave for school. As soon as I left the house, I really woke up.
>
> The dream was so realistic and I guess that's what surprised me the most. I wanted so much for it to be true but I knew it was just my imagination playing tricks on me. I was disoriented. I had to think for a second if my mom's death was a dream. Then I realized that my mother was gone for good. The dream made me feel weak. I felt like I lost a huge part of myself and now there was an empty void that would remain with me for the rest of my life. The dream made me realize I had been in denial about her death. It was as if the dream was a wake up call. I knew I had to come to terms with the whole situation. The dream made me aware that I couldn't depend on my mom any more. Before she died I thought I was a tough guy, but after she died I realized how vulnerable I was. I was without a mother. I didn't know how I was going to make it through each day without her support. I wondered why the dream was of her serving me breakfast. It made me think maybe I wasn't missing her so much as missing what she did for me. I do wonder who is going to fill her shoes. Ever since she died I have tried to replace her with my aunts and girlfriends. I guess I'm looking for the love and warmth that my mom used to give me. I guess the dream made me realize that I had a lot of stuff to work out for myself before I could be of any use to anyone else.

Frank's dream offered a view of where he was in the grieving process. He had been in denial, yet he had been subconsciously seeking to find substitutes to fulfill the needs his mother had met. Frank came to see all the challenges presented by his mother's death, and went into counseling to help find better ways of adjusting.

Guilt

The circumstances of a death affect the intensity of the grieving process as does the quality of the relationship. In the following dream, both these factors are apparent. Qiana was thirty-four at the time of the interview and her mother had been forty-three when she died of cancer.

She had lung cancer. She had smoked for years and years. She actually stopped smoking two years before she died. She didn't know she had cancer. She had a persistent cough and finally went to the doctor and he found it. It was the same day the Space Shuttle exploded. I can remember the whole country being upset about the Space Shuttle exploding and I was watching it on TV thinking that I didn't care because my mother was dying. I wasn't part of the national grief because I had my own personal grief. Six weeks after the doctor found the cancer, she died. She went really fast.

I've had different versions of this dream, and I've had it a lot, but they are the same scenario. I'm in the old house where I grew up. Mom comes back, and says she had to pretend she was dead, but she really wasn't dead. Now she wants to step back into her role as mother. I said, "Where have you been? What do you mean that you're back? You've been dead all these years. I've taken over; I've handled all the money." She always asks me, "Where is all the money?" And I say, "What do you mean? You didn't leave us that much! John had this much and I had that much." She tells me she wants a full accounting of all the money, and she wants a full accounting of why I let my brother do certain things. She accuses me of letting things happen while she was away. She says she trusted me to take care of things.

The dream left me confused. I was happy to see her, but angry that she pretended that she was dead and that she expected me to run everything the way she would have even though I was still young. I was in my twenties when she died, but I felt like a kid. And so the dream scenario is that she comes back and she shakes her finger at me and accuses me of not doing a good job and I get angry at her and say, "You know, you're dead." Lately, I've been saying, "This is just a dream. You're not really back," so I'm sort of taking over the dream.

The way I understand it is that, being the oldest I felt this huge responsibility fall on my shoulders. I didn't have time to plan for it. I was too young for the responsibility, and my mom had very high expectations of me. Suddenly, I have a twenty-year-old brother, who looked to me as his mother and my eighty-year-old grandmother who looked to me as a daughter. The dream is about this guilt I felt that I didn't fulfill my mom's expectations. The thing is, my mom, if she had been alive, would have absolved me. But the ghost of my mom is not the actual woman. For example, I was surprised at how standoffish she was in the dream. When I told her how happy I was to see her, she said, "We'll have time for that later; this is what I want to know now," and we never got back to the other stuff. Instead she laced into me. "I want to know how you made all these decisions in your life; how could let your brother do all these things? I thought I taught you better than that. I thought you were going to take charge." The dream related to my life. I was the oldest and came from a family with an alcoholic father. What do they say about kids like me? They are the over-achievers. It doesn't matter if I achieve something. I still feel that I fall short of the mark. So the dream related to how I view my own life because I still feel I come up short, no matter what. That's why the dream kept coming back. When I was a teenager, I never got to be angry with my mother because we had to get away from my father. It was my brother, my mother, and me against my father. So, I couldn't be angry with her because she saved us from him. I think I was getting around to it when she got sick and died, so I never got to say to her, "You know, your expectations of me are too high." In the six-week period between diagnosis and death, she really lost consciousness and was in great pain. There was no good time with her. There were just responsibilities for me. I even had to tell her that she was dying; the doctor wouldn't tell her. So, I never got to work any of that stuff out with her. We never became adult daughter to adult mother. I had just graduated from college, so she never got to see me as an adult on my own. Since I never got to say those things to her while she was alive, I think the dream was giving me an opportunity to confront her in my dream. My mom has been dead ten years. My progress has been slow. No one ever asked me about stuff like this. I mean, it's not the sort of thing you do, calling people up and saying, "I just had this really disturbing dream about my mother. Do you want to hear it?" I mean, who wants to hear about your dreams anyway?

The dreams began ten years after Qiana's mother died. At that point in her grief, Qiana could understand the unresolved issues in her relationship with her mother. The dreams revealed these insights to her and led her to accept the truth of their relationship. Among those who dreamed of their mothers, 48 (30%) said the dream produced thoughts of regret. Another 24 (15%) said the dream made them feel guilty.

The next dream also deals with feelings of guilt. George was fifty years old when he related this recent dream of his mother who was sixty-eight when she died from cancer. He had the dream about a week after she died.

In the dream, I was sitting at the kitchen table in the apartment where I used to live. My mother walked into the room. She was wearing a large hat and a flowered dress. She looked healthy but concerned. She came right over to me, sat down next to me and put her arm around me. I had been very depressed. She said to me, "Son, you're not taking care of yourself. You should be doing better than this." It was so real. It didn't seem like a dream. I said nothing. My eyes filled with tears and I cried, while she held me. Everything got blurry and I woke up crying.

The dream left me feeling very sad and terribly guilty. I thought how my mother didn't get to see me or her grandchildren very much. I didn't go visit her much or take my kids to see her. I remembered how I never took her complaints seriously. I never inquired about her health. I never knew she was sick until I got the call from the hospital. I think the dream told me that I procrastinate a lot. No, it's more than that. It showed me I didn't care about her like I should have. I was only concerned with taking care of myself and lately I wasn't doing that too well. Now as I'm talking about it, I realize I don't go see my own children as often as I should. It was a disturbing dream.

This is an insightful dream that looked back at George's relationship with his mother. It revealed the painful reality of his self-centeredness. It showed him that this pattern continues in his relationship with his children. At the time of the interview, George knew he didn't like what he saw about himself in the dream, but didn't know if he could change. He said he wanted to change but wasn't sure he was ready.

Guilt figures prominently in the next dream. Radha was thirty-one at the time of the interview. Her mother had died suddenly from an aneurism at the age of sixty-three. The dream occurred nine years after the death.

> In the dream, we were sitting on a couch together, but I didn't recognize the place. I had no idea that she was dead. She was visiting and we were chatting although I don't remember what we talked about. We were just having a great time talking. What I do remember is that my mother gave me a hug and a kiss and said goodbye and walked away. I had the same dream over and over for weeks. Every time I was dreaming, I felt so happy because I had no idea that she was dead. At the end of the dream, she was walking away and I was begging her not to go. I would cry for her to stay with me. I would actually wake up sobbing.
>
> The dream made me remember that our last conversation before she died was not a good one. I had to go to Delaware on business and she literally begged me not to go. I went anyway. I lost my patience with her on the phone and said I'd call her when I got home. I never did. I came home tired and went right to bed. The guilt will always be with me. To this day, it's unbearable to think about this. The dream told me it has taken a long time to let go of my mother and that I still haven't forgiven myself for what I did.

We all fall short in our loving relationships, so grief usually has some guilt. When someone we love dies after we've had an argument or disagreement, this guilt is difficult to manage. Learning to accept that we are morally flawed and to forgive ourselves is not only needed for working through our grief but also for becoming more tolerant of others.

Loneliness

Loneliness, the feeling of absence, of an aching hole in life, is central in the next dream, but other feelings accompany it. Sylvana was twenty-five years old. Her mother died from cancer at the age of fifty-seven. Sylvana had the dream three months later when she was twenty-one.

> In the dream, it was a nice bright day, possibly before noon. I could tell this because of the sunlight coming through the windows. I saw my mom. I knew she had already passed away. Now she was back in the bedroom we

shared. She hugged me but when I tried to hug her back, my hands would go right through her. She looked healthy, not sick. She told me that she knew that I was lonely and she wanted me to know that I was not alone because she was always with me and watching out for me. She was sitting on our bed and I knelt in front of her and put my head on her lap. I could feel her run her fingers through my hair and tell me that it was okay. She told me "You're not alone. I'm still here and I sleep next to you in the night like always. I love you very much." I again tried to touch her but she told me that only she could touch me; I couldn't touch her. She hugged me and told me that I would be fine, that everything would be okay. One last time, she reassured me, "You're not alone." Then she hugged me, said goodbye, and just faded away until she completely disappeared.

After the dream, I felt really good because I got to see my mom again; I actually felt her touch. It was so real. Then the loneliness returned. Ever since she died I've been lonely, like there was a part of me missing. A big part of me died when she died. I think it is hard for anyone to understand this unless they experience such a loss and even then it's never exactly the same. With my mom I felt safe. She was my protector and with her I felt I could do anything; nothing was impossible. I was still angry because life was so unfair. She was a wonderful woman, not just because she was my mother, but because she was a wonderful person to anyone who knew her. I know it's wrong, but I used to get very jealous and envied people who still had their mothers living. I wouldn't wish that they were dead, because my mom would not want me to do that, but I got so angry; I felt like I'd been cheated. The dream made me realize that I was lucky to have a mom like her. I guess it was my mom's way of getting through to me. Doing this interview brought back the actual dream. It is amazing how real it was. I still remember the dream from beginning to end. It's as if I had the dream yesterday and not four years ago. If I talk about my mom, really talk about her, I cannot do it without getting upset. I guess you never get over the loneliness. You might be able to get used to it, but the hurt never goes away.

This is a clear expression of the pain of loneliness which is often part of grief. Among those who dreamed of their mothers, 71 (45%) said the dream made them feel this sadness. Sylvana's dream has a consoling message, but she still misses her mother. The dream helped her see exactly what she missed – the sense of safety and security her mother gave her as well as the confidence that "she could do anything." Adjusting to the loss of such a person and finding others who could do this for us are great challenges, often never fully accomplished.

Among those who dreamed of their mothers, 101 (65%) said the dream made them realize how much they missed their mothers. The next dreamer was one of them. Tina was twenty years old and recently dreamed of her mother who died one year before. Her mother died at age thirty-five from cirrhosis of the liver.

In the dream, I was with my mom and we were in the village. There were a lot of people and stores, and it was during the day. She held my hand and smiled a lot at me, and she had a glow about her. It felt so real. I was like a little kid, all amazed and surprised to see her. She asked me where my brother was, but I didn't know. We looked around and finally saw him in McDonald's, sitting at a table and eating with friends. We started walking after we found my brother. We walked and talked just like old times. Her hair was black and long; she had an off-white dress on, and she looked beautiful. She looked like an angel. We held hands and I felt really close to her. It seemed to be the present, but it was the way it used to be; how I wanted it to be now. I felt so happy, so close, so safe when she held my hand, and I was taken away into happiness by her glow.

After I woke up, I felt so sad. I missed the little things we used to do, like walking together, shopping, holding hands. I missed that feeling like she was protecting me. I thought that the dream was her way of telling me that she's still with me, not physically, but mentally. I thought she was telling me to go ahead in life even without her. I also remembered how beautiful she was; her smile was so beautiful. Even though she's not here and we don't do the little things mothers and daughters do, I believe I'll always have a mother and she'll always be there for me. The dream told me that I was very lonely and still not ready to be an adult and not have my mother guiding me, but it told me that I have to go on and she knows I can do it. I still miss her but the memories and dreams help to stop the loneliness. Also I believe she is always by my side protecting me and I don't have to worry. Part of me says she's dead, but part says that she's alive. I'm glad I had the dream. I really felt warm and protected in it. It also made me look forward to the end of my life when I'll be with her again.

Although there is no explicit message in the dream, the presence of her mother in the dream had a strong healing effect. Tina recognized her need to adjust to the death, "to go on." She thought that the memories she had of such a wonderful mother as well as the dream with its implied message of continued presence alleviated the loneliness. However, she still looked forward to being reunited with her after death. That's where she was in her grief.

The age of the bereaved also affects the grief. When a child loses a parent, the adjustments can be very difficult and have effects that last all through adult life.[28] It is common for children to have thoughts of dying in order to be with a deceased parent. Virginia was twelve when her mother died during an epileptic seizure at the age of thirty-five. Virginia had this dream twelve years later.

In the dream, someone telephoned me and told me my mother wanted me to call her. He gave me a phone number to call. I tried to explain to the caller that I couldn't call my mother because she was dead. The caller just hung up. Later, when I was in the kitchen of my house, I tried calling the number and my mother answered and started yelling at me. She was angry because I hadn't called right away and she had been waiting for the call. She said, "You believed everyone who told you that I was dead but I am not dead." Suddenly, the scene changed in the dream and I was walking up a mountain trail, but still talking on the phone to my mom. Then I was standing at the top of the mountain looking out over a green meadow. I told my mother that I missed her so much that I wanted to be with her, but she said I couldn't because I have things to do here before I die. When I woke up, I felt very peaceful.

The dream helped me to realize that spiritually my mother will always be with me. At the time of the dream, I was severely depressed and was thinking of ending my life. The dream made me believe that I do have a purpose for being here and I started searching for what that purpose might be. It motivated me to get connected to the spiritual world so I could find my mission in life. This interview was the first time I talked about the dream without getting criticism. After telling my family about the dream and hearing their negative responses, I just kept all my dreams secret.

Virginia, like many dreamers in the survey, expressed disappointment about not finding receptive family or friends who would listen to the dream or accept her interpretation. This delays the healing process for the bereaved. It also weakens the relationship with the family members and friends who disappointed the dreamer.

After a death due to Alzheimer's disease

In the next example, Wanda found the dream helped her understand her reactions to her mother's death due to Alzheimer's disease. Wanda was forty-two years old and she dreamed of her mother one month after she died at age sixty-five.

I dreamed it was the morning of the funeral. We were at the funeral home and it was time for us to leave for the church. We went up to the casket to say our last goodbyes and I watched them close the casket. It was after they closed it that I heard my mother moaning the way she used to in the nursing home. I started screaming, telling people that she wasn't dead and that they had to open the casket. The funeral director insisted that she was dead and I was simply hearing things. I remember crying, sobbing, and protesting that they shouldn't bury her. I kept telling them she was still alive, but she couldn't tell us because she had lost her speech long before she died. They were making a terrible mistake. I felt very upset after the dream. It made me feel frightened and helpless. I was also curious why I should dream something so dreadful and not something happy where she was concerned. I was angry that no one listened to me in the dream, not even my father who knew that she couldn't speak. He had been her advocate for such a long time and now he seemed to give up without fighting.

The dream made me imagine how awful it must have been for her to have lost the ability to speak. I remembered when she was first losing it, she would become frustrated. She would say she was stupid. I used to look at her in her wheelchair with her eyes staring up at me and ask her if she missed us as much as we missed her. It had been so long since I had heard her voice. I couldn't remember what her voice sounded like. As she progressed to the next level of the disease, we used to say we can live with her like this if she remains like this. We were always ready to accept her as she was as long as she was with us.

I miss her so much, but the dream made me realize we haven't had her with us in the true sense for a long time. The dream reminded me how things had changed since her death and how difficult it was to adjust. For such a long time I was needed by her. I would travel every weekend to care for her. For over a year, I'd be with her every Saturday and Sunday from 10 A.M. until 7 P.M. I would talk to her about what was happening in our family. I would wash her hair, put on make up, give her a manicure, and fuss over her. I read to her and we listened to music or watched the TV shopping shows. Now she was gone and when the weekend came, I felt I had no purpose. The dream made me realize I needed to feel needed. My mother had satisfied this need for a long time, but when she died, I felt empty. I am the oldest of three girls and I took care of them. They called me, "Sarge" because I needed to control things. I was not able to control my mother's disease. I was upset that I couldn't stop the progression of the disease. The dream showed me that my dad was willing to let her go because he knew it was best for her. The dream reminded me that a short time after her death he told me that now it was time for me to focus my caregiving on my own family. I guess the dream was telling me that also.

The dream opened Wanda to the insight about her need to be needed and how it affected her reactions to her mother's death. The dream offered Wanda an opportunity to be more self aware and showed her the adjustments she needed to make.

Did you hear me say, "I love you?"

When someone we love dies, it is common to wonder if they knew how much we loved them. The following dream is an example of this. Herman was thirty years old when his mother died from cancer at age sixty-four. He had the dream eight months after her death.

I dreamed my mother and I were in the house where I grew up; we were in her room, sitting side by side on her bed. I knew she was dead, but I was haunted by the question of whether or not she heard me say, "I love you," when I visited her in the hospital the last two weeks of her life. She had been in a coma and didn't really respond so I never knew if she heard me. So in the dream I asked her if she heard me, and she said yes and we hugged and cried together. She said she was glad I had been there.

When I woke up, I felt very happy. The dream answered the question I had been carrying around for eight months. Her answer made me feel great. The only thing is that I wish I'd told her I loved her when she was alive and healthy instead of waiting until she was on her deathbed to say those things.

Herman's regret was a common regret among the dreamers in the study. Dreams like this serve as warnings to the rest of us not to take time for granted. Tomorrow is never guaranteed. To avoid such regrets, we should act today and tell those we love how much they mean to us.

Unresolved anger

There are many kinds of unresolved issues that can haunt people after a death of a parent. The next dream is an example of unresolved anger. The dream comes from Yvonne, a forty-five-year-old woman who related a dream she had about her mother many months after her death of heart failure, at the age of fifty-four.

> I dreamed I was sitting on the bed in my aunt's bedroom. My aunt was sitting next to me and my mother was sitting in a chair opposite us. It seemed like we had already been talking for a while. I was upset. I kept asking my mother why she had given me to her father's family, to be raised by my aunt, and not allowed me to stay with the rest of the family. My mother didn't answer but just looked down at her feet. She seemed to want to rectify her neglect, but wouldn't explain anything to me.
>
> When I woke up, I was emotionally drained. It made me think of the many unresolved questions I wanted her to answer. It reminded me how I have only inherited negative things from my mother—high blood pressure, asthma, and ulcers. None of my siblings have these problems! The dream made me realize I am still stuck; I'm still holding on to my anger. I should be further along in life without still holding onto the past. The dream showed me that the anger is still there. I was the second child and the only one to be given away. After I'd been given to my aunt, my mother had more children, but never came to get me. I've gone for counseling, but the sessions leave me in a deep depression for days afterwards. I appreciate this interview. I think it made a difference in my outlook. Some of the pain seems to have lifted. I know I have to let it go.

Finding a way to let go of our anger—to forgive—is difficult. Realizing we need to let it go is one thing; finding a way to do it is quite another. Some recommend that grievers like Yvonne try to widen their points of view by imagining the millions of people who are like her and that she pray that she and they all find a way to let go and attain inner peace.[29]

The next dream also reveals unresolved conflicts in the parental relationship. Mary was a fifty-four-year-old woman who dreamed of both her mother and father one week after her father died at age eighty-seven. Her mother had died a few years before at age eighty-three.

> The dream took place in the house I grew up in. I was in a large pretty room. My parents were both there and looked very good. (When they died they both looked bad.) It was so good to see them looking so well. Then suddenly I really didn't want to be with them. Something changed and I didn't like being there. I think it was a disapproving look from my parents. In the dream, I was fifteen years old. (When I was that age, I had a lot of conflicts with my parents. They sent me away to a boarding school where I was very unhappy and wanted

to come home. They were very upset about that, so I did what they wanted me to do and stayed there.)

I woke up upset. The dream made me remember my years growing up with them. My father was a minister and brought me up very strict. He was very loving and used to bring me things. My mother didn't like that and told me I didn't deserve them. She also would tell on me if I was late and my father would give me a beating. I knew he loved me because he would give me warm hugs, but I was confused. If he loved me, why did he beat me? I was afraid of his beatings and would hide from him in my room. He had a belt that he used to beat me. I would try to do the right thing, but he always found me wanting; there was always something wrong with what I did. My mother loved me but she was not affectionate. I think she prevented me from getting close with my father. When they got older, and I moved out, I had to go see them. They never came to see me. Just when I started being able to talk with my mother, she died. What surprised me in the dream were the strong opposite feelings I had towards my parents. I still have the same dream. It tells me I still have unresolved conflicts with my parents. The interview questions brought things out of me that surprised me when I heard myself say them.

The dream didn't lead to full resolution of the conflicts but it did make Mary more aware of the relationship she had with her parents. Remembering is a key element of grief. Before we can accept the way a relationship was, we need to have it clear in our mind. The dream triggered the kind of reminiscence that makes it possible.

Goodbye

Blanca was a fifty-two-year-old woman whose mother died of a heart attack at age fifty-eight. Blanca had the dream many years ago but only three months after the death.

I dreamed I was in a train station with my five month old daughter and I saw my mother. She was sitting on a bench up against a wall. She looked peaceful, completely serene. I ran over to her and we hugged and I let her hold my daughter. When I asked her what she was doing there, she told me her train would be arriving soon to take her "wherever." I think she meant heaven but she didn't say that. She quietly but determinedly told me she was all right and at peace and that I should not be concerned about her but take care of my daughter and family.

When I woke up, I thought of how her sudden death left no opportunity for goodbyes. The dream helped to bring closure. It made me feel good to be there with her and my daughter whom she really never got to know. At the time of the dream, I was looking forward to going back to work. The dream made me look at my priorities. I realized my job was not as important to me as my family. It made me realize how important it was to tell those I cared about that they were special to me. Since the dream, family gatherings have become very important and I sense her presence whenever we have a family get together.

The dream also affirmed my belief in an afterlife, one that is peaceful and filled with the loving presence of those we care about.

Among those who dreamed of their mothers, 76 subjects (48.7%) said the dream led them to believe that the deceased was okay.

Visits

Paul was a fifty-six-year-old man whose mother died at the age of eighty-nine. The dream occurred two months later.

> In the dream, I was awakened by her about three in the morning. I heard her call my name; I sat up in the bed and it appeared as though she was sitting on my bed. I couldn't see her entire body, but her face was very clear to me. At first I was frightened because of one of our last conversations before she died. She had told me that when she was ready for me, she would come and get me. I didn't know what she meant at that time, so when she appeared that night, I thought she came to get me. Actually, she never spoke about that. She reminisced about things we had done together and we laughed about them. She asked about my sisters and brothers. It was so real. We never touched one another, although we did when she was alive. Other than that, she was not out of character. She was exactly as I knew her and we talked just as we always had. The dream was probably fifteen minutes but the visit seemed like it lasted for hours.
>
> The dream made me believe that I'll always have my mom. It also made me think that when I die I will be able to visit my loved ones. I also wondered if she only appeared to me. The dream made me feel very good about myself and our relationship. I believe the affection we had for each other will go on forever.

In this dream, Paul is reminded of wonderful memories that he shared with his mother, but the dream goes on to another element of grief, spiritually redefining the relationship in light of the death. Paul believed he would always have his mom, not just in memories but in spirit, for he believed his mother's spirit really visited him in the dream.

The next dream is similar. John was twenty-five years old. His parents died tragically in a car accident when the father was forty-five and the mother was forty-three.

> In the past seven years I have had the dream three times. It always occurs around a graduation. It occurred when I was eighteen and about to graduate from high school. It occurred when I was twenty-two and about to graduate from college. And it occurred recently when I was about to receive my MBA. In the dream, I saw both of them, sitting in the auditoriums. My father was taking pictures of me receiving my diplomas. Afterwards, we had lunch with friends and then I hugged them goodbye.

When I woke each time, I felt both happy and sad. I was happy to see them but sad that they weren't there physically. The dreams made me think that at the times of my accomplishments, they are there to celebrate with me. Wherever they are, they are proud of me. The dreams reinforced my belief that there is life after death and although those we love are not physically present, they are present spiritually. My parents died returning home after visiting me at my boarding high school. In the dream, they are wearing the same clothes they wore on that visit.

Still with me

Here are two dreams from Kevin, a thirty-three-year-old man who dreamed of his mother two weeks after she died at seventy-two of complications during surgery to remove a cancerous part of her lung.

In the first dream, I was at my mother's house in the kitchen having a normal conversation with her. I felt weird because I knew she was dead, yet she was alive in the dream. I kept carrying on the conversation but in my mind I kept saying she should not be here; she is not alive. I wanted to tell her that she died but was afraid because I did not want to hurt her or make her feel bad nor did I want the dream to end. I felt as if she did not know she was dead. Finally, I blurted out, "Mom, don't you know?" I paused because I was afraid that if I said it she would start crying. But she finished the sentence for me. She said, "I know I died." Then I began to cry and said, "Mom, you didn't make it." My mother came around the table to comfort me. We were holding each other and she was telling me that it was okay and that I shouldn't cry. Things got fuzzy after that.

The dream left me feeling comforted. She was so calm about being dead that I got the feeling that she was at peace. The dream made me think about life and how I was taught to understand it. It raised a lot of questions in my mind about reality, and what is real. Even though she is dead and not with me physically, I believe she is still with me in some way.

Kevin had a second dream three weeks later.

In the second dream, we were traveling around the city not talking about anything specific or going anywhere in particular. We were just hanging out together. She was smiling and happy. There was no mention of being dead. It was like it really didn't matter. She was alive in the dream and we were enjoying each other's company.

After I woke up I continued remembering wonderful times we had together in the city. It made me realize how close we were. Just because you can't feel or touch someone doesn't mean she is not real. Someone can still exist through the dreams and memories that you have of them.

These two dreams helped Kevin adjust to the change in his relationship with his mother. Because his mother died during surgery, he needed to know she was okay with what happened and the dreams gave him that. The dreams triggered memories of their relationship and also helped him adjust to how she would continue to exist because he still needed her to remain a part of his life.

Warning about health

In the following dreams, the dead mothers issue warnings to the living that prove to be accurate. The first two focus on the dreamer's health. Lenny was a forty-nine-year-old man whose mother died of cancer at age fifty-seven. He had the dream eight years later.

> When she was alive, my mother was always getting on my case about my weight. She kept telling me that I was too heavy and should lose some weight. The summer I had this dream I had gained more weight. I started feeling sick, but put off going to a doctor. Then one night, I had a dream in which she came to me and told me to go to the doctor right away. She told me she knew I wasn't feeling well. She yelled at me, "You are sick! Stop putting it off! Stop procrastinating!" My mother was a very strong-willed person and in the dream she gave me that look that was very familiar.
>
> The dream scared me and I called the doctor the next morning. I went to the doctor and he discovered I had fluid in my lungs. I had pulmonary edema. I had to go on a diuretic so I could relieve this problem. That was only one of the problems he discovered. He repeated what my mother had said, that I had to take better care of myself. Otherwise I would die and end up there with her. In the dream she had told me it was not my time to be there and she didn't want me there yet. The dream led me to make some real changes in my life, health-wise. It convinced me that my mother is still looking out for me.

Among those who dreamed of their mothers, 92 (59%) said that the dream led them to believe the deceased was watching over them.

The next dreamer is not only warned but given a prescription. Christine was a thirty-five-year-old woman whose mother died of a stroke at the age of forty-two. Christine had the dream four years later.

> I was very sick at the time. I needed help but I don't like to go to doctors and my mother knew that. I dreamed I was asleep and she woke me from my sleep and tried to pour some medicine in my mouth. I resisted her and she wasn't able to get it into me. I had the dream four nights in a row. On the fourth night she again offered me the medicine saying, "Here, swallow this. It is good for you." Then she told me what herbs were mixed in the medicine. I swallowed it and woke up.
>
> My mouth had a funny taste as if I had really swallowed something. I called my grandmother and told her the dream and the names of the herbs mother had told me. Later that day, my grandmother prepared the mixture and gave me the very same herbal medicine. Since then, I have enjoyed perfect

health. The dream showed me that my mother is still watching out for me and that makes me feel really safe.

Not all warning dreams are so direct and clear. Dierdre was forty-seven years old. Her mother died of a stroke at age sixty-four. Three weeks later Dierdre had this dream.

In the dream, my two sisters, my brother and I were walking down a dirt road when we heard a car coming. We observed an old house on the left hand side of the road, so when we heard the sound of the car we ran and hid. The car slowed down and stopped in front of the house. I peeked out to see who was there and I saw my mother getting out of a black limousine. I whispered to my brother and sisters that it was our mother. They were scared and remained hiding. I was the only one who went out from the hiding place. My mother saw me and ran to me and hugged me. She invited me to walk with her down the road. We walked a long distance until we got to an intersection. Then my mother told me to cross over to the other side of the road and walk in front of the church that was there. She held me by the shoulders and looked into my eyes and said, "Make sure that you go to school tomorrow." In my mind I replied that I don't go to school, but my mother repeated her instructions to me. "Make sure that you go to school." Then she said, "Walk in front of the church and don't look back. I'll be back again to visit you." As I walked away from her I did turn around quick to look back, to see where she went, and I saw the black limousine pulling away slowly. This was the end of the dream.

When I woke up I was relieved and excited to have seen my mother. I also felt comforted that she had come to visit me as I missed her, and was glad to see her in the dream. I remembered how much she loved me and thought that she was still looking out for me since the dream was meant to be a warning. At the time of the dream, I had been pregnant but suffered a miscarriage and the doctor had performed the necessary procedure. I had been given a follow-up appointment, but decided not to go. Part of the reason was the additional expense. When I thought about the dream in relation to my life, I saw it was meant to be a warning. I should return to the doctor (my mother had said "school") or there would be serious repercussions. I followed my mother's advice and returned to keep the doctor's appointment. The doctor discovered that in spite of having done a D & C, I was still pregnant, but it was an ectopic pregnancy. I was immediately admitted to the hospital and underwent surgery that same evening. If the tube had ruptured, I could have died. The idea that my mother's spirit came back to warn me of the danger I was in was incredible.

Marital Warning

Emily was forty-two at the time of the interview. Her mother died at the age of sixty-two from a brain hemorrhage. Emily was twenty-eight at the time of the death and had the dream three months later.

I had left England, where I lived, to come to New York City when my mother died in her apartment there. I had to stay several months to take care of her affairs. In the dream, I was in my mother's New York apartment when she and her friend who was also deceased walked in on me. They told me they couldn't stay because they had to go back to England to take care of some of my things. I assured them that my things were okay. My mother looked stern and said, "No, they are not! Your husband and his mistress and her child are living in your apartment and making a mess of things." Then they left.

When I woke, I was shocked by what they had said. I decided I would return to England without warning my husband. When I arrived home, I found things just as my mother had said. In fact I found them in bed. There were cigarette burns on the furniture, clothing and linens. Many of my dresses had been worn by the woman and thrown in a pile in the corner. I threw the three of them out of the apartment and began divorce proceedings immediately. The dream was so real. It convinced me that my mother continues to look out for me.

Continued maternal support

A mother's support and encouragement are important. The next three dreamers thought their dreams indicated that support continued after their mothers' deaths.

Sophia was thirty-seven years old. Six years earlier, she dreamed of her mother, who died at age sixty-eight from heart disease. The dream occurred a year and a half after her mother's death.

In the dream, I was in a large room with glass walls. My former boyfriend was in the room and I was afraid of him. I turned and saw my mother outside, looking at me and I felt she was telling me, "Don't worry. You are not with him now. Everything will be okay."

When I woke up, I felt a great sense of peace come over me. I had just started a new relationship about one month earlier and was frightened. My former boyfriend was my first intimate relationship and he treated me badly. It took me a long time to leave him and my mother had been a great support. I've dreamed of him in the past whenever I felt insecure, especially when I was in a relationship. In this dream, my mother told me that I'm not a failure. What's in the past has passed and I can move forward and love this new man. My mother gave me the support I needed at that time and I did marry him and he is my husband today.

Diabetes was the cause of death of the mother in the next dream. Gwen was thirty-three years old. Her mother died at age sixty-eight, and the dream occurred one year later.

In the dream, I was lying on the bed and could see her sewing on her sewing machine in her room. She looked healthy and beautiful. I never saw her look so good. When she saw me looking at her, she got up and came into my room and sat on my bed. She asked how I was doing and about her other children. She also asked about my new relationship. I was answering her questions when the phone rang and woke me up.

The dream was comforting. I felt happy she was still concerned about the family. I remembered how my mother would always be at the sewing machine during her free time making clothes for me, my two sisters and brother. My father died when I was ten. At the time of the dream, I was planning to get married and was really upset because my mother wouldn't be there to support me. The dream told me she would be with me whenever I needed her support.

Sometimes the mother in the dream offered more than words of encouragement. Allison, a fifty-five-year-old woman, told of a dream she had two months after her mother died of a heart attack at age seventy-three.

In the dream, I was in my house and my mother came in and stood by the door. She had her hands on her hips and she told me she knew I was having some financial problems and that she wanted to give me some money. I started to politely refuse, but she insisted I take it. She then handed me a wad of money with a rubber band around it. Then she disappeared.

When I woke up, I felt so happy to know she was still aware of what was going on in my life and still wanted to help. So the next day I played the lottery with the number of my mother's old home address and I won $5000. This convinced me that she is still looking out for me.

Here is a dream in which the dreamer believes she received support from her mother about giving birth. Janice was forty-one years old at the time of the interview and her mother died at age eighty-six from Parkinson's disease. She had the dream six months later.

In the dream, it was late at night and something woke me. When I cleared my eyes, I saw my mother standing at the foot of the bed. No words were spoken by either of us. I just felt my mother was really there to comfort me and let me know that everything would be all right and I was not alone.

Prior to the dream, I had been praying about my situation. My husband had two daughters from a previous marriage and didn't want any more children. I was now pregnant and my husband refused to accept the pregnancy. Our marriage was under a lot of stress. The dream was very comforting and left me with a great sense of peace about the situation. The dream gave me strength. It reminded me of the qualities which my mother tried to instill in me. The dream told me my decision to go ahead with the pregnancy was the right one, and God blessed me with a beautiful baby boy who at the age of one and a half years is the apple of his father's eye.

Did I make the right decision?

One of the most difficult things an adult child may have to do is make health care decisions for one or both parents. Ideally, the parents make their wishes clear to their children beforehand, and fill out advanced directives like

Living Wills and Health Care Proxy Forms. Too often, this is not the case. Making the decision not to resuscitate is very difficult and will leave the adult child second guessing the decision. In the following dream, the dreamer is reassured by her mother about her decision.

Amanda was a forty-year-old woman whose mother died from lung cancer at age sixty-two. She had the dream three months after she died.

> I worked as a nurse at a hospital. When my mother was dying of lung cancer and was comatose, I made the decision to sign a "Do Not Intubate" (DNI) order. My mother went into respiratory arrest and died. Afterwards, I had feelings of guilt and pondered over and over if I had made the right decision. In the dream I was sitting with my mother in her bedroom. I was changing the sheets on the bed. In my dream, I knew she was dead. I was telling her that I did not know if I had made the right decision to sign the DNI. She told me that she was very happy where she was and that I should not feel guilty. She said that I had made the right decision.
>
> When I woke up, I felt nervous and jumpy at first. I was surprised that I had such a dream. I thought I was finished dealing with the death of my mother and the dream brought it all back. Later, as I thought about it some more, I felt comforted and relieved knowing that my mother was happy and free from suffering. Being a nurse, I knew she would have ended up dependent on a respirator. In my head I knew she would not have wanted to be kept alive that way, but the dream reassured my heart that I had made the right decision.

Blessed assurance

This last dream is interesting for what the dreamer believes it reveals about the afterlife. Lillith was a forty-seven-year-old woman whose mother died from cancer at age sixty-two. Lillith had the dream one month later.

> In the dream, there was a party at my mom's old house. She was there with my father and my aunt and uncle all who had died before her. There were other family members there who are still alive. Everyone was talking, laughing and having so much fun. It was as if they were all still alive.
>
> When I woke up I felt very happy and peaceful. The dream made me think that when I die I will go to a very pleasant place where I will be with all my family and friends again. I usually don't remember my dreams but this was so vivid. The dream told me I have nothing to worry about. I have no need to fear death. My parents are looking out for me and when my time comes, they will be there waiting for me.

Lillith's dream expressed a belief about the afterlife that is very old. There is scientific evidence that the earliest humans, thousands of years ago, believed that they somehow survived death and continued to exist in some form and that when they died they would rejoin those who had died before them. This is a very old and persistent belief that shows up in the study of dreams about the dead.[30]

Chapter 4: Dreams about Fathers

There were 187 dreams about dead fathers (17.6%). Traditionally, fathers were expected to provide material support for their children's basic needs. They were also expected to protect them, providing a secure environment in which they could grow. Today the expectations for fathers have increased to include other needs. After the death of a father, a review of how well or poorly he measured up to the expectations of the adult child is common. Dreams retrieve memories that help the dreamer obtain a clear idea of the relationship and then to find an appropriate emotional response.

The first dream expressed the dreamer's sense of frustration over an unfulfilled relationship with his father. Peter was forty years old and his father died of cancer at age sixty-three. He had the dream within days of the funeral and has had it many times since.

> In the dream, I was on the farm where I grew up and which I took over after his death. I was standing outside the house, enjoying the sunset. Then I noticed my father's silhouette at the edge of a field. The shape was so familiar. I knew it was him. I walked towards him, but as much as I walked, I never got any closer to him. It was like a rainbow; as I moved in his direction, his image kept moving further away. I realized I couldn't reach him, so I stopped. I shouted to him but there was no sign that he heard me. I never got close enough to see his face.
>
> The dream left me feeling frustrated and hopeless. After thinking about it more, I realized the dream was similar to our relationship when my father was alive. I kept trying to reach him, but we never connected. He wasn't a talker; he just took care of the farm. He left parenting to my mother. I was never happy with my relationship with my father. I guess I never will be.

Among those who dreamed of their fathers, 20 (10.7%) said the dream pulled up negative memories. After a death, there may be an awareness of painful, unsatisfied needs in the relationship. Peter was still struggling with the lack of intimacy in his relationship with his father. He didn't believe there was any way that he could come to accept the way it was between them, but there are ways. This dreamer might benefit from group counseling or a support group in which he could learn this is not something that he alone suffers. He could come to understand that his father was probably following the model he had received from Peter's grandfather.[31]

Memories

The next dream came from Malachy, a sixty-two-year-old man who dreamed of his father who died of congestive heart failure at the age of eighty-five. He had the dream about one year after the death.

> I was in the military in Europe and on leave to my home in Ireland. After a few days, I was departing for Berlin. My dream began with my departure. My father accompanied me to the local village where I went to school and spent my former years. We went into a pub in which there were a number of people. The owner greeted us with enthusiasm. The bus that I was to travel on was leaving from outside this pub. We were just there to talk; father was in great form. He moved close to me and gave me a drink and said, "This is for the road." In a little while, the bus stopped outside, so I gave my father a hug and went out and stepped onto the bus. Then I woke up.
>
> The dream left me feeling sad and tired. It reminded me of those days when I was younger and my father was very much part of the family. My mom died when I was only eleven years old. Dad, with the help of my older brother and sisters, kept the family together and we were very happy. During my childhood almost every day was spent going to the village and buying ice-cream with dad. During the months of July and August much time was spent together in the bog preparing the turf for the winter fires which kept the house warm and cozy. The dream was about saying goodbye to dad, not knowing when or if I would see him again. It made me feel sad. The dream revealed to me hidden thoughts and feelings that are deeply imbedded in me. That was a surprise!

Among those who dreamed of their fathers, 68 (36%) were surprised by something in the dream. Dreams bring to our consciousness important memories and feelings that keep us connected to the dead and show us more clearly who we are. Many times they surprise us.

Insights

Nick was a forty-nine-year-old man whose father died unexpectedly at age fifty-three, right after he was discharged from the hospital after his initial fight with cancer. The dream didn't happen until twenty years later.

> I dreamed I was asleep in my bedroom. Something woke me up from sleep. When I opened my eyes, my father was standing by the foot of my bed. Oddly enough, I was not surprised to see him there. I was more concerned with my worries about my recent diagnosis of cancer. I was worried about who would take care of the kids when I died. I turned toward my father and he was shaking his head as if to say, "No. It's not your time yet. You will be able to take care of your kids." That was all there was to it, but it was very real.
>
> The dream left me feeling comforted. It instilled in me a gut feeling that I was going to survive. After that dream, I was able to focus on getting better, so I could be there for my kids. Before the dream, I had thought of little else than what would happen to them when I died. The surprising thing was that I never had a good relationship with my father, and we were not on good terms when he died, but he had the power to comfort me when no one else could. In retrospect, it is also surprising that I gave so much clout to the feelings that I came away with from that dream. It was only a dream, but again, it had the power to comfort me when I could not be comforted by anything or anyone else. The dream made me realize I had it in me to survive. In retrospect again, I think I had been harboring feelings about my father and other people in my life. Once I started to let go of those feelings, I had more energy to focus on my recovery.

The dream could have been considered a message from the dead but Nick gave it a psychological meaning. The power to survive didn't come from outside him but from within. He also discovered the healing power of letting go of negative emotions.

Although the next dreamer finds some spiritual elements in the dream, she primarily values it for showing her that her feelings toward her father are not all negative. Margaret was a thirty-six-year-old woman whose father died of a ruptured small intestine due to acute alcoholism. She had the dream twenty years ago, but only two weeks after he died, the day after she went to identify the body. She was fifteen years old and lived on the island of Jamaica.

> In the dream I was outside my house, cooking bananas. It was right after sunset. Suddenly I heard him behind me, asking me in a critical tone, why I was cooking so many bananas. I turned around and realized the voice was coming from the prepared grave site. Then I saw him; he looked just the same as when I identified the body. He had dried blood at one corner of his mouth. He was standing there looking at me. I was terrified and turned and ran. He ran after me. I ran into the house, went upstairs and through the house. He continued to run after me. He was yelling, "You know I don't like bananas yet you still cook

them." When I reached the porch and turned around, I tripped. As I fell, I saw him reaching to grab me. Maybe he was reaching to grab me to stop me from falling; maybe he was grabbing for me for some other reason.

When I woke up, I was scared and wondering what he really wanted from me and what he wanted to say. I believe he was actually there in spirit. After the dream, my mother told me not to be afraid because he will not hurt us. "He loved us too much to hurt us," she said. Maybe that's the reason why I had no more dreams of him, because he realized how much he scared me. The dream also left me with regrets. He was upset with me in life and he was upset with me in death. Maybe I did not stay to listen to what he had to say. I did that also when he was alive. When he was dying, he did not get to say goodbye to me because I was not there when he died. Maybe he had something to say to me and the dream was his way of trying to do it. He was trying to tell me something and I ran. I don't think he is at peace and that bothers me in a way. I don't think that he was happy with the way he died. This interview was good because I was able to rethink my relationship with my father. I think I am still grieving all this time. The first time I heard that my father was dead, I said, "Finally. Good." He wanted to die. He had a death wish because his life was not going the way he wanted it to go. In terms of getting respect from the people around him, he was getting less respect because of his addiction. He was losing everything because of the alcohol. Now I understand what addiction can do to people. But at that time I did not understand. I saw him as a terrible person when he drank. But when he was not drinking he was the nicest father one could ever have. He was really nice. Even though he was terrible sometimes, I wish he was still alive.

The dream moved Margaret from an extremely negative image of her father to a more balanced view. She put it this way, "I wish that we had had a better relationship before he died. He stayed drunk most of the time so we did not have time to work at our relationship."

Here's another insightful dream. Noreen's father was sixty-eight when he died after a fall. She was thirty-six when she had the dream three years later.

My father was picking fruit in a tree, in his yard. He was stung by a bee and fell off the ladder and hit his head. He died of complications secondary to head trauma. I dreamed I was in my bed, looking out the door towards my children's rooms. In the hallway, I saw the figure of my father coming out of my son's bedroom. Then he peeked into my room and said to me, "Nice house." He didn't say anything about my children. I need to tell you that he had never met my son because I was seven months pregnant with him when my father died. He was in my son's room, and came out of the room to tell me that I had a nice house! And then he walked away, and that was the end of the dream. I remember in the dream I got up to look for him, to see where he went, but he was gone.

The dream really disturbed me. I always felt badly that my father never got a chance to meet my son. When he said, "Nice house," and didn't mention my baby, I was angry at him. The fact that he was coming out of my son's room made me think that he was checking on my son. It bothered me for a long time. I always felt guilty with the relationship I had with my father. It was far from ideal. Then he died of a traumatic injury rather than a slow illness, so there was a lot of unfinished business between us. The dream reminded me of this. I was disappointed that the dream was so short. I wish I could've said more to him, or he had said more to me. I remembered, in the dream, I was thinking about why he was there because I knew he was dead. It wasn't realistic. Well, it was and it wasn't. While I was aware that my father was dead, he looked like he was in perfect health. He acted normal, the way I remember him. He was charming and polite and didn't say very much, but usually when he did say something, it meant something. I remembered how just a few days before he had the accident, I had an argument with him. It was something silly, but we never resolved it. I think the dream showed me that I still think fondly of him. My house was a new house. That's why he said, "Nice house." He had never seen my house. I was trying to figure out why he would say "Nice house," rather than, "Your children are beautiful." The dream showed me that I am a worrywart. I've always worried about something. I worried about death. Sometimes I've said that there's no life after death, but I don't know what I think. I think, in some way, the dream showed me that he's looking out for me. He came, he made a visit, he checked everything out, he said, "Nice house," and he left. And that's very to the point. Get your business done; that's the way he was. The dream showed me how I read into things a lot. Rather than seeing the dream as a visit and being thankful that he's looking after me, I am nitpicking and thinking about what he didn't say. It's funny that it's just such a short dream, but it just will always be with me. I remember it vividly. Every detail was in place. It was very real.

Feeling the loss

The following dream was triggered by the dreamer's pregnancy. Odette was a thirty-nine-year-old woman whose father died in a drowning accident when she was fifteen. She had the dream eight years later when she was pregnant with her first child. She had the exact same dream three years later when she was pregnant with her second child.

I dreamed I saw him going into what looked like a house. I followed him, but when I went into the house it looked like a bar but actually was not a bar. I did not know the other people there. I never said anything to him and he didn't say anything to me, but our eyes met and he smiled at me. That was it, but it was like I really saw him. I was right there with him in the same room. I found myself somewhere with him.

The dream left me feeling sad. I really miss my father. I think I had the dream because I was soon to give birth. I was not far away from the due date. I think that that is the reason. I was wishing that he was still around, but he wasn't. I never really thought about that until just now. I was pregnant at the time and excited about becoming a mother. I wished that he might have been around to see his grandchildren. I really feel bad that he is missing all the important events in my life.

Odette understood the dream to be an expression of her sense of loss, of the absence of her father from when she was only fifteen, of the empty space in her life that she wishes her father were filling. This painful emotion overshadowed the pleasant surprise of having a vivid encounter in her dream. The dreams were triggered by the expected births of her children.

He's really dead

Patricia was twenty-one when she dreamed of her father one year after he died from cancer.

> I dreamed it was around Christmas time. I was home alone and the phone rang. It was my father. I knew he was dead, so it was really weird. I thought someone had recorded his voice and spliced it all together to make it sound as if he was really talking even though it wasn't him. Whoever it was then played it to me. The voice was saying that it had been a mistake and that he was really alive. I kept saying that whoever this is on the phone better stop because it wasn't funny. After I hung up, I began looking for my family. I went to my mother's office and to my brother's school but couldn't find anyone, anywhere. Finally I gave up looking and went back home. Everyone was standing in the living room, including my father. It was a happy, joyous homecoming with everyone hugging, laughing and crying. After hugging him, I asked if he had called and he said no. That's when I woke up.
>
> I woke up very sad, realizing my father was really dead and there would never be such a family reunion. I woke up crying and I don't cry often. The phone call thing was really weird and disturbing. The dream told me I still wasn't accepting the fact that my father had died.

Among those who dreamed of their fathers, 68 (36%) said the dream made them realize, to a greater extent than before, that their fathers were really dead. Also, among those who dreamed of their fathers, 90 (48%) said the dream put them in touch with the sadness they still had inside. In addition, 121 subjects (64%) said the dream made them realize how much they miss their fathers.

Letting go

Rhoda was a forty-five-year-old woman whose father died from cancer at age seventy. She dreamed of him two years later.

> In the dream I was in my mother's house walking to the dining room when I noticed another room, like a banquet room. There were lots of people standing

around in groups, talking. I noticed my father talking to a group of his friends. His back was to me, but I recognized his suit. At first, I was glad to see him but then I realized he and his friends were all dead. My father turned toward me and smiled and gestured with his head, meaning "What's up?" Meanwhile I was scared and panicked and turned to leave as fast as I could. He caught up with me to see what the problem was. I started to cry and told him it was because he was dead and wasn't supposed to be there. He didn't touch me but said if I couldn't handle it then maybe he hadn't done such a good job of raising tough kids who could handle anything. I said, "No. You were a great father but I really miss you." He told me he was okay with his death and I should try to be too. He was happy with his friends and that was fine. He said to me, "Rhoda, let it go."

When I woke, I was crying. It was so real. It was like I really was with him. I miss him so much but what he said really struck me. He did raise me and my brothers to be tough, not to let things get us down. When he said, "Rhoda, let it go," it really got to me. I knew I had to accept his death. The dream made it easier by showing me he's okay with it and is in a good place. It was so real!

Rhoda loved her dad very much, and he loved her. They showed their love with lots of visits and phone calls. She craved to have more of these expressions of love from him. Death requires a big adjustment, giving up this deep desire that things be the same. Rhoda realized she had to stop using so much of her emotional energy pining for her dad. That was the tough adjustment required to handle his death

The next dreamer also needed to make adjustments, but the circumstances were quite different. Ozzie had the dream fourteen years after his father died. He was forty-one at the time of the interview, but a young adult when his father died of cirrhosis of the liver at age sixty-two.

I dreamed my mother and I were out walking in a strange neighborhood and we stopped at a bar. When we entered, we were so surprised to see my father was the bartender. He, too, seemed surprised when he saw us but greeted us warmly and asked us what we would like to drink. We both asked for coffee which he served us. Then we talked. My mother and I asked a bunch of questions and he explained to us that he did not die but that he had to go into hiding and he had been working as bartender ever since. The dream just seemed to fade with us sitting at the bar talking to him. Then I woke up.

At first, I felt good that he was alive, but then I realized it was only a dream. The dream made me realize that I had been denying the death of my father for many years. The dream made me remember that my father was an alcoholic. I recalled how as a child I had often wished my father would just "go away." Then, one day, he did not come home. I remembered feeling happy that my wish had come true. When the police told us he had died, I did not want to accept the fact that he would never be coming back. The dream seemed to be about giving me a second chance so that my father and I could work on resolving the issues between us. The dream made me realize that a lot of my personal problems go back to my dad's death. As a result of this dream, I went to see a counselor. At this point in my life I have begun to accept that my father is dead and that it was not my fault.

It is common for children, like Ozzie, to think they were responsible for the death of a parent whom, at times of conflict, they wished would disappear or "go away." They need to learn that their wishes did not cause the death of the parent, that they are not bad, and that they don't have to be tortured by a secret guilt.[32]

What might have been

Rachel was forty years old when she described how her father died of lung cancer at the age of sixty-five. She had this dream sixteen years after his death.

> I dreamed I was a child again and visiting a friend. My father was outside in his car, waiting to drive me home. I left my friend and walked to the car and asked him what he was doing there. I said to him, "You're not supposed to be here." I knew he was dead but I hugged and kissed him anyway. He felt so real physically. I was very happy to see him. I could smell how he smelled; I could feel how he felt. He didn't look any older and he looked healthy.
>
> After I woke up, I felt so sad. The dream was so real and he seemed so real that seeing him stirred up all my sadness from his death. I realized how much I still missed him. The dream brought him closer to me, but only for a short time. It left me with a great feeling of emptiness. I thought about how he doesn't know what I'm doing anymore, what I've become. I still have good feelings about him from my dreams. I love seeing him in my dreams and having the chance to hug him again. I've had other dreams of him and they are always positive. Sometimes I feel protected by his spirit, but most of the time a sense of void overcomes me. I feel empty because I realize the dreams are not real. I would have liked to have known him better. I was only in grammar school when he died.

Rachel's relationship never had a chance to develop. Her sense of loss is based more on what she wished might have developed rather than what their relationship actually was.

No one will ever take his place

Stacey was nineteen years old. She told how her father died of liver failure at the age of forty-seven. She had the dream three months later.

> You need to know that when my father was sick, he stayed in the front room of our house. In the dream, I went into that room and was surprised to see him sitting there. He told me to sit down with him and we started talking. It was so real. I was telling him what was going on in my life and suddenly I realized

he was dead. I asked him about it and he got very silent. He looked sad and then he faded away.

When I woke, I felt very sad. I couldn't believe he was not still alive. I don't know if he was a ghost in the dream or just a figment of my imagination. Maybe I didn't want to face the fact that he had died. The dream reminded me of all the unanswered questions I had and still have. I have a lot of questions about life and I want them answered by somebody. I want to have the relationship back that I had with my father when I was young, before he got sick. No matter what I did, I could talk to him about it. Ever since he died, I can't seem to find someone like that. I really, really miss him.

Stacey clearly expressed how difficult it was to make the internal and external adjustments after the death of someone who meant so much to her. She recognized what it was her father did for her, and seems to be looking for someone to fill in for him, but she has not found anyone yet. It might be that her ideal replacement is just that—ideal. It is common that we idealize the dead. This makes it difficult to find people to fill in the gaps in our lives.

Here's a dream from another young woman whose father died when she was a teenager. Theresa was a twenty-one-year-old woman who dreamed of her father three and a half years after he died from cancer at age fifty-four.

In the dream, three of my friends from college and I were driving to Boston to meet our families for a football game. When we got to the stadium, we discovered that we had really good seats, right on the field. Our families were already there and that included my father. I sat next to him and he put his arm around me and asked me if I was warm enough because I was only wearing a sweater and a windbreaker. We were talking about school and joking around. He then told me that we were at this particular game because the band, U2 was there and we were going to meet them. I started to get nervous and my father calmed me down. I remember him saying that they were only people and they were no better than me. He really made me feel better. So we went to talk to them (just me and my dad) and they were really cool. After we left them, my father said, "I told you they were just regular guys." The dream ended with my father hugging me goodbye. Then I got into my car to drive home and a horn started beeping because I was in the way. It was really my alarm clock beeping.

When I woke up, I felt warm, happy, and a little sad. It made me realize how much I missed telling my dad my problems and hearing his soothing encouragement. The dream was very real. I could smell my father's after shave as he sat next to me. I had the dream the night before U2 concert tickets went on sale. The dream told me that I miss my father and that no matter what is going on in my life at any period of time, he'll always be a part of it. I think that dreaming about my father is either a way of remembering him or it's an actual communication with him.

Theresa seems to have adjusted to her father's death. She still misses him but has learned to manage without him. She also has learned to live with uncertainty – whether or not the dream is a real spirit communication or a wonderful creation of her memories and imagination.

Guilt after a suicide

The next dream revealed to the dreamer the conflicted feelings he had towards his father who hanged himself. Ray was twenty-seven years old when he told of the dream he had about a year after his father's death.

> I dreamed that I was running up the stairs to get to the roof. Somehow, I knew that my father was going to kill himself. I thought if I got there in time I could save him. I got to the roof and opened the door and just at that moment, I saw my father with the rope around his neck, still standing on the chair. I called out his name and he looked at me and then fell off the chair. By the time I got to him, it was too late; he was dead.
>
> The dream left me feeling very guilty. It reminded me that my father had tried to get in touch with me before he died but wasn't able to get me. If I had been there I know he would not have done it. I thought that maybe if I had not moved away from home, he would not have gotten so depressed and hanged himself. I felt bad that I hadn't been there for him the way he had been there for me. What was surprising about the dream was that he heard me and turned to look at me but didn't respond. It also seemed that he lost his balance and fell off the chair. This made it more of an accident than a suicide. As a result of the dream, I no longer blame myself for my father's death. Maybe if I stayed at home or if he were able to get in touch with me, things would have been a little better, but not completely. The dream helped me see that. It also showed me that what I say and do can have a big impact on other people. I have to be more careful and consider how my words and actions may affect others.

Those who are in grief over a death by suicide face two strong emotions — anger and guilt.[33] The survivors are usually angry at the deceased for taking his or her life. They also feel that they were somehow responsible. Among all those in the study, there were 28 cases of death by suicide. Among these, 43% said the dream made them feel angry and 46% said it made them feel guilty. In the case of Ray, before the dream, he suffered greatly from feelings of guilt. The dream enabled him to gain a new perspective on the events and a more balanced evaluation of what happened.

Apologies from beyond the grave

In the next dream, the father apologized to the dreamer. Wendy was fifty-one years old when she related how her father had died of a heart attack at the age of forty-nine.

I dreamed I was sitting in my room at night and my father appeared before me. He was wearing the same clothes he had been buried in. He looked very sad. He knelt down in front of me and asked for my forgiveness. It seemed as if he couldn't have peace without my forgiveness, so I told him that I forgave him. He smiled, kissed my hands and disappeared.

When I woke up I was surprised by the dream. It was very real. It had been twenty years since my father died. The dream reminded me of my childhood and how much I disliked him. Actually, I hated him most of my life. Then I imagined what he must have been suffering. The dream asked me what kind of person I wanted to be. Did I want to be the kind of person who held grudges against everyone who injured me? Did I want to be a generous, forgiving person? I figured that everyone deserves to be forgiven, including my father. The dream left me feeling peaceful.

When we hate someone, we are bound to that person by negative emotions. When that person dies, the grief includes dealing with those emotions. Forgiveness does not come easy or quickly. It took Wendy twenty years to get to the point of letting her anger go. The dream showed her that she had reached that point in her grief.

The next dream also features an apology. Alice was twenty-one years old. She dreamed of her father two months after he died of liver failure.

In the dream, I seemed to be somewhere between heaven and earth. I was sitting at a table in what looked like a lobby of a hotel. There were other people there, but I didn't recognize anyone. It seemed to have been a place for people to meet with the dead. I heard a door open and when I looked up, I saw my father walking towards me. He sat down near me and we started talking. He asked me how I was doing and said that he was proud of me. Then he looked sad and said he wanted to apologize for leaving me when I was young and then dying a few years later. He then explained what had been going on in his life back then. The dream ended with us saying goodbye again. It was a little sad.

When I woke up I felt sad that he was dead, but I felt better because he took the time to explain what had happened and to apologize. The dream made clear to me how unhappy I had been with the way things ended and that I needed my father to explain clearly what had happened. The dream left me feeling very comforted.

Among those who dreamed of their fathers, 76 (40%) said the dream gave them comfort. The cognitive pain of grief consists in part of seeking to under-stand the way someone died, or why they died, or in Alice's case, why her father left her when she was young. The dream went very far in relieving Alice's pain by providing her with understanding. And the apology relieved the pain from the anger she had held against him.

Messages from the dead

Elaine was thirty-two years old. Her father had died of a heart attack at age seventy-two. She had a dream about him, eighteen months later.

> I dreamed I fell asleep sitting up in bed. He came in my room and sat in a chair at the foot of the bed. He sat in his usual position, a hand on each knee. When I woke in the dream and saw him, I was disoriented. I said, "Dad, is that you?" He smiled and nodded. I asked him how he was and he said he was fine. I said, "You left us so suddenly." He apologized and said, "I know it was a big shock to you all, but I went quietly and peacefully just how I always wanted to. You've all done a good job with the grave. It looks great but I have to tell you something. It's very funny to see you standing around the grave, looking down at it as if that was where I am. I want to tell you, I'm up here, above ground. I can't tell you how funny it looks." Then he said, "You are all worried about your mother." (This was true. She was going in to have a hip replaced.) "She will have her operation and do fine afterwards." I asked him if he was happy where he was and he said, "I'm very happy. I'm up here with my mother and father and two brothers and I have a grandchild up here." Then he said that he had to leave and was gone.
>
> When I woke up, I felt very warm and comforted. As I reviewed the dream in my head, I couldn't figure out who the grandchild was. The next day, I told my husband the dream and he reminded me that I had a nephew who died one month after birth from congenital deformities. It happened ten years earlier and he never left the hospital. I think my father was trying to tell me not to worry so much about my mother and to know he was happy and we should let him go and accept his death. It was a wonderful dream.

Elaine's dream is a good example of a dream that has many meanings. First, she found a message not to worry about her mother's upcoming surgery. She also believed the dream was evidence her father was spiritually alive, not "down" in the grave. In addition, Elaine thought the dream meant he was happy and not alone. He was with loved ones, including a special grandchild. He had a life there and he needed to get back to it, as she needed to get on with hers.

Critical messages

Connie was thirty-eight years old when she related her dream of her father. It occurred about twelve years after he died at age thirty-five.

> I was back at my father's funeral, sitting in the viewing room of the funeral parlor. Suddenly he got out of the casket, walked over and sat down next to me. He started a conversation about how I should have been doing better than I was. At that time, I was in a bad relationship. He referred to it and said, "Come on, Connie, you know this is not right for you. I had to come all

the way down here to straighten this out! Couldn't you have seen this on your own?!" He shook his head slowly and told me that I should know better than to be doing some of the things I was doing. He said, "You were taught and raised better than that." Then he stood up, gave me one more serious look then kissed me on the cheek and was gone.

The dream left me feeling really good. It made me believe that my father was looking out for me. He was trying to bring something to my attention that I was doing wrong. I imagined he was up there in heaven looking down on me, and he saw that I was messing up badly. He probably said to himself, "My daughter needs my help." The dream made me look hard at the relationship I was in and made me realize that I deserved better. As a result of the dream, I did get out of the abusive relationship and changed some other things as well. I don't want my father to have to straighten me out again!

Connie interpreted her dream to be an example of a message dream that was meant to correct her. Connie was open to taking the advice because, in the dream, she sensed her father's love and concern.

The next dream is similar in that it gets the dreamer to reevaluate her priorities. Dahlia was forty-two years old. Her father died of heart failure at the age of sixty-two. She had the dream three months later.

Due to immigration laws, I was unable to attend my father's funeral. In the dream, I was coming home from work in the evening. After I entered my apartment, I heard him calling me. It sounded like he was in a closet. He was saying, "Let me out. Please let me out." I opened all the closets but couldn't find him. I shouted, "Where are you? Please answer. I can't find you any-where." He kept calling me and I was crying when I woke up.

The dream scared me. It made me wonder if there was something I should have been doing for my father. It brought back memories of him and my family and I felt lonely. I realized how much I missed them. At the time of the dream, I was away from home and wasn't keeping in touch with them. The dream made me realize family is more important than school or work or anything else and that no matter what, I should have found a way to get home and attend his funeral. I regret that now, very much.

I feel relieved in openly discussing the dream. I have always felt embarrassed about it and have never shared it with anyone before. I don't feel as guilty as I was feeling before the interview. The questions made me think a lot about the meaning of the dream. They helped me sort out my feelings about my father. I will visit his grave and apologize for not attending his funeral. I believe he will understand and forgive me.

Dreams about the dead are opportunities for the bereaved to process their grief. What the dreamers need is for someone to let them talk about it without judgment, but with compassion. Then, as in Dahlia's case, elements of her grief that had been suppressed, surfaced, meanings were found, and things to be done were revealed.

Messages about health

Fatima was fifty-two years old. She dreamed of her father twenty years after he died.

I dreamed my father was standing outside my house, calling my name. I hurried out to greet him. He said he came back because he had something to tell me. He asked me to take his hand and he took me to the place where he said he lived. It was a mosque where people were dressed all in white and were praying. He turned to me and told me that he knew I was suffering from a chronic illness and that the medicines weren't working. He told me the reason I had health problems was because I was not praying five times a day and living according to the Qu'ran. He promised me that my health problems would cease if I listened to him and changed my life.

When I woke up, I thought of how much I was suffering and how the doctors weren't any help. I remembered how much my father had loved me and how he had lived his life as a good Muslim and hadn't been sick at all in his life until he died suddenly of a stroke at age sixty-nine. So, I started to follow his advice by praying everyday and reading the Qu'ran. I stopped drinking alcohol and eating pork. Little by little my health problems disappeared. I was surprised that my father, who was dead for twenty years, knew about my health problems. It felt wonderful to know he still cared about me.

In the next dream, the father was also concerned about the dreamer's health. Bonita was fifty-eight years old. Her dream occurred two years after his death at the age of ninety.

In the dream I was back home in Peru. I was standing near the pier where my family used to set up a stand and sell the catch of the day when I was a little girl. It was late in the day because I remember the reflection of the sun on the ocean. I saw a group of people. They were family members. One of them was my father and another was my brother who died twelve years earlier in a car accident. My father walked over to me and hugged me. He asked me how I felt. I told him I was so happy to see him. He said he was glad I was happy but he was asking how I felt physically. I told him I felt fine. He looked at me seriously and said I had to take better care of myself and look after my health. He made me promise to go see a doctor for a check up. Then he hugged me again and walked back to where my brother had remained standing silently. They both turned around and walked away with the others. I tried to follow and I called to them, but they looked back and waved goodbye. I raised my hand and woke up crying.

The dream made me feel strange. I felt guilty because I was stubborn. I always refused to go to doctors. The dream disturbed me, but I thought I was fine and was not going to let a dream get to me. But I had the same dream every night for two weeks until I finally went to a doctor. Then the dreams stopped. I was glad I went to the doctor because I learned I had very high cholesterol, but with medication I've been able to bring it down. So the dream taught me not to be stubborn and not go to doctors, also not to take my health for granted and finally, to be more careful about staying healthy. The dream left me feeling very happy knowing my father and brother were okay and together and that they were still looking out for me.

Bonita thought her dreams had two main levels of meaning. She felt comforted knowing her father and brother were okay and looking out for her. The dream also revealed her obstinacy about not going for medical check ups and taking her health for granted.

Offering financial support

Fathers often support their children financially. Some dreams indicated this support continues beyond the death. Gina was thirty-nine years old. Her father died of heart failure at age sixty-two. She had the dream one year later when she was twenty-eight.

> I dreamed I was visiting my father in prison. I was upset he was there and asked him why he was in prison. He was calm, like at peace with things. He smiled and said, "I'll be here for seven years and fifteen months." That was all he said to me! Then I woke up.
> I was perplexed. My father had never done anything to warrant him serving time in any prison. Then I felt sad, realizing he was dead and how much I missed him. The dream brought back memories of my father and the last time I saw him. Then I remembered how my father was a pretty frequent numbers player. In the dream, when he gave me the length of time that he would be incarcerated for, he gave it in a very peculiar way. I wondered why he didn't say eight years and three months instead of seven years and fifteen months. Out of curiosity, the next day I enquired about what number won. It was seven-one-five. I thought that the dream was telling me that my dad was watching over me and trying to give me a few dollars. It also told me I would never get rich from gambling!

Here's a good example of how dreamers find a meaning in a dream that, on the surface, made no sense. Gina believed that the strange dream was a message from her father and the fact that the number seven-one-five was the lottery winner the next day proved to her the meaning was correct.

Watching over me

Steve was thirty-three years old. He dreamed of his father four years after he died from cancer at age seventy-five.

At the time of the dream, I was in Europe on a business trip, away from family and feeling alone. I dreamed I'd just arrived at some kind of function with a lot of friendly people. It was like a party. People were moving about greeting each other. What happened next was quick, a fleeting moment but very vivid. My father suddenly came up to me. He was wearing golf clothes with plaid golf pants and a salmon shirt and a big straw hat. He came up to me and said, "How are you doing? I just wanted to check to see how you were." I was caught completely off guard and just managed to say, "I'm okay." I was about to ask him how he was, but he had waved, turned and was gone.

I woke up laughing and shaking my head in disbelief. It felt like it was a real visit and was very comforting. It made me believe he was watching out for me. I believe my dad is in a better place, walking a golf course, having fun. And I think that being dead isn't such a bad thing, so I shouldn't be afraid to die.

Heidi was thirty-eight years old. Her father died of a heart attack at age sixty-five.

It was a lucid dream. By a lucid dream I mean that I was very actively involved in the dream. There was a lot of activity, a lot of people and dialogue. At one point, when I became aware that my father was there, then at that point it became a lucid dream. I was watching the dream and saying, "Oh! There's dad. What is he doing here in this dream? He doesn't have anything to do with it." The thing about the dream that was curious to me was that I was aware that I was seeing someone in the dreaming state who was not alive. So that realization is what brought me out of the dream. From then on, what was going on in the dream at that time didn't matter. The focus became that he was in the dream and he was as I remembered him before he died. He was very much the same and he had been dead for seven years, and yet it was absolutely as if he had not been dead. The look, the sound of him, the way he was dressed, everything was absolutely real with absolute clarity. There was nothing fuzzy about him. When someone has been dead for a long period of time, we forget a lot of things about them, like how they used to jingle change in their pockets. We don't usually remember that but when they come back, they come back absolutely in the right context. He even smelled like my father. And he was just being my father. He was not participating in the dream; he was not talking; he wasn't doing anything. But he was absolutely there and I was aware of him and it was so real, it was as if he was still alive. It was as if he were there because he was interested in what was going on in my life, just sort of watching.

The dream made me think that there was no separation of time between the past and the present. The dream also made me think about the relationship between the waking state or the every day state and the other reality that you know in the dream state. My father was so real in the dream it was as if he could reach out and touch me. It was absolutely that real. It made me believe that, in fact, there is no differentiation in time and that everything is happening at the same time. In the dream state you slip in between the different worlds. In the dream, he and I seemed to be in the present not the future or the past.

This is an example of a lucid dream. Lucid dreams are those in which the dreamer realizes he or she is dreaming and has some control over the dreaming process. Once Heidi saw her father in the dream, she realized she was dreaming and focused exclusively on her father. The powerful dream experience led her to reformulate her views of reality, especially time.

Sudden death

When someone dies unexpectedly and not of natural causes, the grief of the survivors is usually intense. In the study there were 133 accidental deaths. Here's an example. Tom was thirty-three years old. His father died suddenly at the age of fifty-nine.

> Before he died, my father fell in the bathtub and broke a rib. He went to the hospital and the doctor told us he would be home in a day or two. The day before he was to come home the doctor called and told us he had died. I had this dream two weeks later. I was in my parents' house and it was very dark. I was downstairs in the living room. I went to the kitchen and then I decided to go upstairs. The only light that was on downstairs was the night light in the living room. I started up the stairs and I could see the night light in the bathroom. As I got closer to the top, I was startled to see my father standing there at the top of the stairs. I remembered thinking he was supposed to be dead. Why was he standing at the top of the stairs? There was no verbal communication between us. My father moved. Either he walked to the bathroom or to the bedroom where my mother was. Then he came back and stood right in front of me again. Then he was gone.
>
> After I woke up, I thought that the dream occurred because I was having a problem accepting that he had passed away. We were very close and I really missed him. I was still upset that he had died. The dream reminded me of how he was in the hospital and I did not go to see him because I expected him to come home. He was in the hospital for two days and he was to come home the next day so I never went to the hospital to see him. When the doctor called and told us he had died, I was in total shock. I realized I never got to say goodbye. The dream gave me the feeling that everything was going to be okay. I felt comforted. I am not the type of person who subscribes to the type of thing where somebody comes back from the dead to talk to you, so during the dream I was looking over my shoulder and thinking, "Is this really happening?" At the time I did not believe in those supernatural types of phenomenon where somebody actually comes back from the dead. But the dream made me feel as though it really happened. Even after I woke up, I thought it really happened, that it was not a dream. This is the first time I ever had a dream with any kind of spiritual significance. At that time, I had so many conflicting thoughts. The dream helped me to straighten them out. I think the dream made me realize that I might be more vulnerable than I let on.

Tom's words express well how powerful the dream experience can be and how it can lead to a change of attitude and beliefs. If he wasn't an unbeliever, he was a skeptic about the spiritual reality of such dreams, that is, until he had a dream, himself. The dream offered insights into his inner state and the conflicts that were swirling around him since his father's sudden death. Among those who dreamed of their fathers, 67 (35%) said it made them think about their beliefs in life after death.

Wanting to dream of the dead

Some people seek to dream of the dead, believing it is a way to make contact. Imelda was twenty-five years old. Her father died from a stroke at age fifty-two. She dreamed of him three weeks later.

> I dreamed I was walking through a strange town with flashes of familiar places. I saw a mob of people walking ahead of me. I could only see them from behind, but I thought I saw my father among them. I caught up with them and got closer to the man I thought was him. He stopped and turned around. It was my father! He smiled, held out his arms and gave me a big hug. Then he stepped back, put his hands on my shoulders and asked, "Are you satisfied now?" Then I woke up.
>
> The dream made me recall how I had been trying to contact my father in my dreams. I finally did! I finally got to say goodbye. It was a great dream.

There are dream courses that claim to teach people how to gain some control over their dreams. Some of them offer techniques for dreaming of dead relatives and friends. Imelda had taken such a course and was ecstatic when she had the dream she wanted to have. It gave her a sense of closure in her grief.

To see him one more time

The next dreamer attained a deeper understanding of his relationship with his father. Vincent was thirty years old. His father died from cancer at the age of fifty-two. The dream came to him five years later.

> I don't know if it was God or an angel, but when I was asleep someone came to me. I thought it was a dream but I couldn't wake up. He or she came down and asked me if I wanted to win a lot of money and be rich, or would I rather see my father one more time. I chose to see my father. Suddenly I was back in my apartment and he was sitting next to me on the couch. We hugged and started talking. We were just talking. I don't remember what we said. The dream ended while we were talking. He was crying and I was crying. He didn't leave. It ended when I woke up.

I really felt good when I woke up. At first when I woke up I thought I really had seen my father one more time. But then I realized that it was just a dream. The dream reminded me of my childhood belief that eventually one day we will all be reunited after death. I felt that faith again that we would meet again somewhere, somehow, and that belief made me feel really good. What was surprising about the dream was that everything was still the same as if he had never died. The dream also showed me that I'm part of my father. I'm part of what my father was.

Vincent had been taught to believe in life after death and that faith was rekindled by his dream and it comforted him. The dream also offered an insight into how much more of his father Vincent had internalized. The same values that had directed his father's life, now directed his.

Requests from the dead

In the next dream, a dead father asks his son to take care of the dreamer's mother. William was twenty-six years old. His father drowned at the age of forty. William had the dream one week later.

I dreamed I was lying on the couch in the living room when he walked in. I was scared and excited at the same time. He said, "Don't worry about me. I'm very happy, but I want you to take care of your mother. She's not doing well." I got up to give him a hug but he put up his hand to stop me. Then he smiled and disappeared. That's when I woke up.

The dream lessened the pain of losing him because I believed he was all right and very happy. It changed my thinking. I used to think that after death you just went into the ground. The dream made me believe there is life after death and in his case it's a happy place. I was disappointed that I didn't get to talk with him but he wouldn't let me. The dream was so real that I'm still not convinced it was only a dream. It convinced me that I had someone who thought enough about me and cared so much for his wife, my mother, that he came back from the dead to ask me to look after her. He was right about mom. She put up a brave front but was really hurting. My father's death had devastated her. So I got her some grief counseling and she's doing better. It's what he would have done. It feels good to talk about him this way. I haven't done it in a long time.

The sudden tragic death of William's father had overwhelmed his mother with grief. She was unprepared for all the adjustments, internal and external that needed to be made. The dream made William more aware of his mother's vulnerable state and he found out the local hospice ran weekly grief support groups that were open to anyone in grief. William said his mother found support and guidance for her grief.

The next dream is similar. Joyce was thirty-eight years old. Her father died from a heart attack at age sixty-eight. She had the dream about one year later.

> I dreamed I was walking up my block when I heard someone coming up behind me. He was running. When I turned, I saw it was my father! As he passed me, he waved to me as if he wanted me to follow him, so I started running after him. I couldn't catch up with him but stayed with him until, after a few minutes, he stopped. When I caught my breath, I realized where he had stopped. We were standing in front of my brother's house. My father was looking at the house and then turned and looked at me. He didn't say a word. He just gave me a sad look of concern. I moved toward him to give him a hug, but I woke myself up.
>
> After I woke, I tried to understand what he was telling me. I remembered how much my father loved and cared for us. I realized he was asking me to help my brother's family who are in need because my brother passed away two years before my father died. My father had been supporting them before he died. Now he was asking me. I felt special that my father came to ask me to help them. And I did and still do.

The last two dreams focused on being aware of the needs of those who are bereaved. Our society underestimates the challenges of grief and so the bereaved often hide their needs, thinking they should be able to do better on their own. The truth is, they need the support of others to get through their grief. Joyce understood this through her dream and acted on what she learned to help her sister-in-law and her family.

Did he suffer?

Among those who dreamed of their dead fathers, 54 (28%) said the dream made them wonder about how the deceased died. Here's an example. Kristen was thirty-seven years old. Her father died suddenly from a stroke at age seventy-four. She had the dream one month later.

> After his death, I pondered whether anything more could have been done for him by the paramedics. The question was on my mind a lot. Then I had this dream. Our family was sitting at the dining room table. My father was in his usual chair. It was dinnertime and all the food was on the table. I was happy to see him but shocked because I knew he had died. "What are you doing here?" I asked. He smiled and seemed calm and peaceful. This was not like him. I asked him about his death, if he had suffered. He told me it was okay, and that there was no pain. I needed to know more. It was very important to me, so he took me to the place where it happened, near where I lived. He explained he blacked out and fell on his face and broke his nose. He comforted me and told me he hadn't suffered and now he was happy and at peace.
>
> The dream made me feel better. I got the call to go to the hospital because he carried a card in his wallet with my name and phone number. When I saw his body at the hospital his nose was broken and his clothing was soaked in

blood, so I felt he must have suffered a lot. Even though the paramedics had assured me that he hadn't suffered, I needed to hear it from him directly. So the dream showed me his death wasn't as awful as I had imagined. His experience was not painful. Now I could be at peace about it. The dream revealed how much I cared about my father. It pained me to imagine him suffering. Now I knew he was in a better place and was happy. Nothing in this life could have made him so peaceful.

When a loved one dies a sudden or tragic death, it is common for the survivors to wonder if he or she suffered. Kristen was tortured by her imagination. The dream put an end to this torture by answering her question in the way that she needed, with assurance directly from her father.

What is life after death like?

Lora was twenty-one years old. Her father died three weeks before she had the dream.

I dreamed I got up out of bed and went into the kitchen where my father was sitting at his usual place at the table. His hands were folded the same way they always were folded. I asked him what he was doing up so late and he told me he was uncomfortable and wasn't able to sleep. This had always been his excuse. He got up to lean out the window and I followed him and did the same as he. We were gazing up at the stars and started discussing space and when the universe started. This is something we always used to do when he was younger. Then, he started discussing death and what happens after death, and how God decides the fate of people after they die. At this point I realized my father was dead and that I was dreaming because we never discussed the afterlife. We never discussed anything like this before. He told me that there's a heaven and that it is a wonderful place. He said that God is fair to all who deserve it and that if I stay the good person that I am, I'll be there with him some day too. He stopped the conversation because he said that I needed to get to sleep because I had to go to school the next day. We both went to our bedrooms to sleep. I looked across the hallway and saw him lying in his bed and then I shut the door behind me and went to sleep.

When I woke up, I felt peaceful because I knew that he was in heaven. I also felt a sense of closure. He was very sick before he died and I never got the chance to say goodbye. The dream told me I must be a good person for my father to trust me and let me in on one of God's secrets – information only the dead have.

The last dream is similar. Andrew was forty-one years old. His father died of cancer at age sixty-six. Andrew had the dream two months after the death.

In the dream, I was in a dark hall and off in the distance I could see a door that was open. I could see a bright light shining from the room and I was drawn to it. As I got closer, I felt a glowing warmth coming from inside the room. When I reached the doorway, I looked inside. I saw only light. It was very bright. I felt a presence in this brilliant room. I was attracted to it, so I went in. The door closed part of the way behind me. I felt strange and realized I couldn't feel my body. I felt embraced by the light and I wanted to stay there. I felt surrounded by love. My mind was racing. I remembered what I'd read about near-death experiences and made a conscious decision to stay in the light. In this light I felt my father's presence. Then I heard his voice. He told me this wasn't my time yet. I felt myself being guided to the door that was almost closed. The door opened and I was guided back into the hall. As I passed through the doorway, I could feel my body again.

When I woke up, I felt I had experienced God's love and my father in the light. I was disappointed that I woke up. I wanted to be back there. I thought that now I know what God's love feels like. The dream made me think about death and how I should not be afraid of dying, now that I know what comes next. The dream made me think about letting go of this body. My father was okay being dead because he wasn't really gone. My father was engulfed by love and it was so good. It was comforting to know that he's in such a wonderful state.

The question of where the dead go and how they are is part of the cognitive challenge of grief. The bereaved often say they could just rest easy if they knew their dead loved ones were all right. Lora's and Andrew's dreams were gifts that gave them peace of mind in this regard. They both felt they had received a glimpse of life after death. Lora was happy she was able to say goodbye to her father. Andrew was happy knowing his father was "in such a wonderful state."

Chapter 5: Dreams about Siblings and Cousins

Siblings have a very different relationship to each other than a child has with a parent. Siblings are from the same generation, formed by the same familial models and experiences, shaped by the same historical and cultural events of a particular slice of time and place. In their formative years, they learned to express themselves with the same words, the same style of clothing, music, and dancing. They understand each other easily and validate a particular view of life. For many cultures and families, cousins are thought of like siblings and considered part of the immediate family, so we include them in this chapter. In the study, there were 77 dreams of dead siblings and 50 dreams of dead cousins.

Reviewing the relationship

Marjorie was twenty-one years old and dreamed of her brother the night after he died of AIDS at the age of thirty-one.

The dream began with me sitting on a bench with my brother on a boardwalk by the ocean. It was the end of a beautiful day. We were talking about old times. Then I began to have flashbacks of all the events that led up to his death. First I was talking to him at the train station after coming from a New York Yankee game. Then I was in a temple celebrating a wedding with family and friends. My brother and I danced together and toasted the bride and groom with champagne. At the time of the wedding we didn't know about the sickness. Then we were at my house. My brother and my dad had just returned from fishing and my mom and I were waiting for them so we could have dinner together. At that time he had HIV, but it wasn't full-blown AIDS yet. Then we were at my house a second time only this time he was with his boyfriend and AIDS had developed. Next, we were at the hospital. He was dying. Finally, we were home in the house when we received the call from the hospital that informed us that he had died. I woke up in tears, depressed and upset. We were very close. The dream made me miss him all the more. The dream made me feel very angry. I was angry with God. I thought that it was so unfair of Him to let my brother die. He was a good person. So what if he was gay! He never hurt anybody. I was also furious with the Catholic Church and what it preaches about homosexuality. The local priest refused to give him the last rites because he was gay. That sealed it for me. The dream brought back all the memories we made together, the good and bad. I was sad at the fact that I not only lost a brother, but I lost a friend. We told each other everything. I confided in him! Now he was gone and I was without my friend. He wasn't going to be there to see me graduate from college or celebrate my twenty-first birthday with me. We planned so much and all that was taken away within a few months. The dream did help me have a better perspective on life. I realized I shouldn't worry so much about tomorrow; I should just take it one day at a time. I believe I should live each day for that day itself. I also try not to take things for granted. The dream showed me that I was lucky to have such a great brother and that I have to be grateful for the time we had together. After the dream, I joined an AIDS workshop where I've been teaching other people about AIDS. It was my own little part in the crusade against AIDS. The dream also made me believe that my brother was okay. He wasn't suffering any longer. He was somewhere out there, free from pain. I'm not certain. On one day, I think he is in Heaven; on another day, I think he is reincarnated.

Marjorie's dream is a good example of the rich texture of some dreams. It involved a review of the relationship; this is an important part of grieving. Many dreamers in the study were helped to do this by their dreams. Marjorie's dream put her in touch with both her emotional responses, both negative and positive, and her cognitive responses. As a result of the dream she also channeled some of her grief into the crusade against AIDS. Finally, the dream clarified the extent of her loss; he was not just a brother but also a friend.

Negative Insights

Nilda was eighty years old. She had a dream two months after her older sister died at the age of ninety-two.

In the dream, we were coming home from a family celebration; one of the grandnieces had graduated from college. We were in my car and I was driving. We were having a nasty argument about someone at the party. As usual, she had to be right and wouldn't listen to my side at all. I woke up so angry that I was shaking.

The dream reminded me of how nasty she was and how we were always fighting about things. Before the dream, I had been feeling guilty about not missing her. The dream was like a guilt remover. It showed me it was okay not to feel guilty about not missing her. The truth was that we never got along well. When she died I felt relieved to be free from daily fighting with her. The dream showed me it was all right for me to feel that way. Some people say you're supposed to love all your family. My sister and I were so unlike in personalities that we were worse off than strangers. She was domineering and always wanted her own way. She was always fighting with someone. She was tough to get along with. I wasn't the only one who felt this way. I'm sure if there is an afterlife, she is fighting with everybody there! It feels good to be able to say this without being made to feel guilty.

Nilda's dream triggered a review of the relationship which introduced more realism into how the relationship really was. There is a tendency for people to idealize the dead, or at least not to "speak ill" of them. This denying of the negative elements in the relationship hinders the grieving process. Fortunately, Nilda was able to realize and accept that the emotional bonds with her sister were primarily negative.

Changing the relationship after death

Olympia was a thirty-six-year-old woman whose brother died of AIDS when he was forty-three. She had this dream two years after his death. There were only 8 interviews in which siblings died of AIDS.

In the dream, I was at some wedding reception and he walked over to me and said "Come on, Baby Girl, let's dance." I gave him a huge smile and obliged. We danced all night long with all our family members watching us. Then I woke up.

The dream left me feeling relieved. I felt like I had done something that I should have done long before. I was surprised to have dreamed of him like this when our relationship was stormy. I had not approved of his lifestyle. This dream made me realize that all the times I had spent fighting with him I should have spent dancing with him. Ever since this dream I feel like I have made a bond with my brother that I didn't have when he was alive. I feel that he forgives me for being so judgmental and is telling me to keep good relations with all the rest of the family.

Olympia's dream is a transformative dream. Her dream changed the fundamental attitude she had toward her dead brother. The dream facilitated the change, for in the dream the brother initiated the change by asking her to dance. Olympia felt this symbolized his forgiveness of her negative judgmental attitude, which she regretted. The dream extended the change to include all her family.

Feelings of guilt

Many dreams addressed the way feelings of guilt linger after a death. Here are three more examples that involve traumatic deaths and include very different ways of responding to guilty feelings.

Paulette was twenty years old. Her sister was hit by a car and killed at the age of five. Paulette was thirteen at the time. She had the dream three months later.

> She and I were in our church in the first pew with a lot of other people; she was crying but wouldn't tell me why. I was hugging her, trying to console her and find out why she was crying but the more I tried, the louder she cried. Then suddenly she stopped and gave me a great big smile. She looked so happy and so peaceful. Then she started to tell me something, but I woke up before she finished.
>
> When I woke, I tried to catch what she had been trying to tell me. I think she was telling me that she was happy and safe where she was. I believe in life after death and that I'll be with my sister some day. Maybe that's what this dream was all about. For a long time, I thought if I had been with her she wouldn't have died. I was supposed to be with her. I didn't want to go to the city that day so I pretended I was sick. So my aunt just took my sister and not me. I've never told anyone that I pretended I was sick. In the dream, I wanted to ask my sister if she felt it was my fault she died because I wasn't with her, but I never got to ask her. This dream made me go over the events and realize I couldn't have prevented the accident. I haven't had this dream in a long time until recently. What was different about the latest version of the dream was that I was my present age in the dream. What was strange was that even though my sister wouldn't have recognized me at this age, she did!

Paulette's dream relieved her of her guilt. She reviewed the events and realized she was not guilty. And so she was able to admit to pretending she was sick.

The next dream has some similarities but the dreamer is still tormented by the guilt. Bob was twenty-two years old. His sister was hit by a car and killed when she was ten years old. He had the dream for the first time, the next night.

> I've had the dream repeatedly since her death. It basically replays the events leading up to her death. If I hadn't gone off our property to hide when we were playing hide-and-go-seek, she wouldn't have run across the street and gotten killed. Every dream feels like it only lasts from hearing her say "Ready or not, here I come" to hearing the car slamming on the brakes and me just yelling as loud as I possibly can for her to stop. I wake up in a cold sweat and crying every time. The dream wipes me out. After the dream I feel terrible. It was my fault and everyone in my family still blames me for it. God is punishing me by making me have these dreams. My life is a mess because of not being able to let go of this. I never know when I might have a flashback or

dream about it so I am constantly on the lookout. Presently, I am seeking professional help. I want to know why I can't get it out of my head.

Many dreams like Bob's are basically replays of the events that trigger the feelings of guilt. Unlike Paulette, Bob believed he did cause his sister's death. Family members reinforced this judgment. Bob's interpretation of the dream is spiritually negative. It is sent from God to punish him. At the time of the interview, he was seeking psychological help, hoping it would free him from his emotional torture. Among those who dreamed of dead siblings, 20% (16) said the dream made them feel guilty.

The third dream, that involves feelings of guilt, comes from Carlos, a twenty-two-year-old man, who dreamed of his cousin who was shot to death at the age of twenty. He had the dream one year later.

It's like it was happening all over again. I was at a party with two of my friends. At first we had a good time but when it got crowded they wanted to leave while I insisted on staying. A little while later a fight broke out and everyone was pushing to get out of the apartment. Some guy pushed one of my friends so I stepped on his boot. My friend kept telling me to forget it but I wanted him to know that I was a big man. We started to argue and then his friends came over to ask what the problem was. So we all started to argue. There were more of them than us so I told them to stay there and I would be back. I called my cousin, who is big, and he came right away. When the four of us went back into the apartment, the other guys just started shooting and my cousin was killed. That's where the dream ended.

The dream really made me feel bad. I felt helpless. I felt like a nobody. The dream made me realize how stupid I was not to listen to my friends when they wanted to leave. I felt it was my fault he died. I still do. It could have been avoided. The dream tells me it won't be long before I get killed too.

The dream took Carlos straight back to the actual events of a year before. The interview reflected his feelings of guilt for his role in the death of his cousin. It also reflected his awareness that his behavior is self-destructive. He hadn't changed his ways since his cousin's death and so, he figured he would probably die a violent death in the not too distant future. Carlos was in need of some psychological/spiritual intervention for his pain. Some would say he was subintentionally suicidal, that is, he was playing a role in hastening his death, although he would deny it.[34]

Hell

Many dreams about the dead reflect the dreamers' concerns about the whereabouts and status of the deceased. These dreamers' interpretations are often affected by religious stories and beliefs which they had been taught. Here are three examples where the dream raised ideas and images of Hell.

Donald was a thirty-year-old man whose brother died of a stroke at the age of thirty-five. Donald had the dream one month after he died.

> I saw my brother in the midst of a great fire. He was in a lot of pain. He was screaming and crying. It was very real and scary.
>
> When I woke up, I thought he must be burning in Hell. I felt bad for him but remembered what I'd been taught about how important it is to live according to God's Will. The dream reminded me of a lot of bad things my brother had done. Then I thought about the way I was living my life and made some resolutions. The dream showed me there is a price to pay for disobeying God's commandments, and that I needed to follow Jesus' teachings more carefully. I've never talked to anyone about this dream before.

Rose had a similar dream with images of the flames of Hell. She was forty-six years old when she told how her cousin died from AIDS at the age of thirty-one. She had the dream one year later.

> In the dream, it was autumn and there was a building on fire. There was a crowd standing outside watching the fire. I looked up and saw my cousin in the building. He was standing in the flames, trapped in the building. He wasn't burning, but he was just standing in the midst of the flames. Someone called out to him and I woke up.
>
> I was disturbed and confused about the meaning of the dream. I thought the dream meant my cousin was burning in Hell. This idea bothered me because he had confessed salvation after becoming a born-again Christian. The dream told me that the way a person leads his or her life is important. It also showed me that you can never know what will happen to a person or how he will spend eternity. That is left between God and the individual.

The last dream like this comes from Susan, a thirty-one-year-old woman whose cousin died from pneumonia at the age of forty-five. Susan had the dream seven years after he died.

> I was in my bedroom lying on the bed, watching television. Suddenly my cousin appeared and jumped on the bed with me. He kept trying to stuff his fingers down my throat. His fingers seemed so black and long and scary. No matter how hard I tried, I couldn't get his fingers out of my throat. Then I felt the bed getting hotter and hotter. I kept fighting him off until I woke myself up.
>
> I woke up terrified. It was so real, but it left me confused. The dream made me remember negative things about him. He did a lot of bad stuff. I thought he must be in Hell since he was making the bed so hot. Then I thought about the direction I was leading my life and my own death and about my beliefs about life after death. I decided I had better make some changes. It was a scary dream.

Dreams like the last three were rare among all the dreamers interviewed. There are many more that indicate the deceased was in Heaven although what the dream revealed about Heaven did not always conform to what the dreamer had been taught about it. Here are some examples.

Other images of the afterlife

The first dream in this series comes from a nineteen-year-old woman, Toni, whose sister died of cerebral palsy at the age of nineteen. Toni had the dream six weeks after her sister died.

> In the dream I seemed to be in the home where my sister spent most of her life. It was a bright and sunny afternoon. I saw someone who looked like her and walked over to see if it was her. As I approached her and realized it was my sister, I was so happy to see her. I was surprised to see how happy and healthy she looked. She was smiling and laughing. That was it. It was short but very vivid.
>
> When I woke, I felt so relieved, seeing she was okay and happy. She had suffered her whole life and I needed to know she wasn't suffering any more and that she was happy in a better place. The dream reminded me of what a strong and special person my sister was. It also affirmed my belief in an afterlife. I believe she is in Heaven, happy and healthy because she deserves it and I wished more than anything that she could have it.

The dream validated Toni's beliefs and confirmed her hopes for her sister.

The next dreamer is Ursula, a thirty-three-year-old woman whose cousin died of a stroke at the age of forty-four. Ursula had the dream one month later.

> I dreamed I was dreaming and suddenly woke up after having fallen asleep at the wheel of my car. In the dream, I looked around to make sure I wasn't driving and saw my cousin sitting in a chair in my room. I knew he had died and asked him what he was doing there. He said, "Nothing really. I've got to wait because it's crowded. I just have to wait my turn." I was really happy to see him and asked him how he was doing. He told me he was all right. "I'm okay. Everything is okay where I am. I just have to wait my turn." Then he laughed and disappeared. That's when I really woke up.
>
> I know it was a dream but it felt very real. The dream showed me there really is something after death. I always believed in the afterlife, but sometimes I would bounce back and forth about it. For a long time, I questioned whether life after death was real. This dream convinced me I definitely have something real to look forward to, although, like my cousin, I'll probably have to wait!

The next dream comes from Victoria, a forty-four-year-old woman whose brother died of a stroke at the age of twenty-six. She had the dream twenty-four years later.

> In the dream, I was eighteen years old again and fixing dinner for the family. My parents were in the house and my three brothers and two sisters

were playing outside. Suddenly my deceased brother appeared in the doorway and asked to have his meal so he could get back to work. He looked very sad. He talked to me and my parents very calmly but seemed unhappy. He said his work was very hard and his boss was very strict. After he ate, he said, "I'm going. I'm late for work. I'll see you again." Then he faded away.

I woke up confused. This wasn't what I'd been taught about the afterlife, but I was glad I had the dream. It reminded me of my brother and the many good times I spent with him and the rest of the family. The dream's meaning was that although he died twenty-four years ago, he is still part of the family.

The dreamer chooses not to dwell on the negative aspects of the dream but to find a positive meaning for the dream.

The last example of a dream with an image of the afterlife comes from Ethan, a twenty-five-year-old man who was the youngest kid in a big family. He had the dream about his older brother ten years after he died of a massive heart attack at the age of thirty-six.

I was in the school yard at my grammar school and I was playing basketball with a bunch of other kids. I was the same age I was when he died, because that's when I was on the basketball team and I was wearing a tee shirt I always wore when I was at basketball practice. So I stole the ball from this big sweaty kid and turned around to run for the other end of the court, but the big sweaty kid came up behind me and knocked me down. He laughed and then walked away. So I was lying there on the ground and I started to pick myself up when someone held out his hand to me. I looked up and it was my brother, only he was the same age as me. I recognized him from his pictures that my parents had up on the walls of our house. So there he was, leaning over me with his hand out to me. So I grabbed his hand and he pulled me up off the ground. He helped me brush myself off and then we ran off back to the game.

The dream reminded me how much I liked the guy. It made me wish I had known my brother a little better than I did. He was married and out of the house by the time I was eight or nine. He seemed pretty cool though. I remember he made pretty good money and for Christmas and my birthday he always brought me stuff that my parents couldn't afford. He was more like an uncle. The dream brought back memories of New Year's Day, when we'd always watch all the football games together, me, him, and our dad. I have tried to be there for his son. He's twelve now. He was almost two when his father died. It's sad that he never knew his father. Even though I didn't know him all that well, I tell him what a good guy his father was whenever I get the chance. I had spent the day before I had the dream with my nephew. That was probably what triggered the dream. I guess the dream answered my question about how my brother was doing. I wanted to know if he was happy because he was always happy when he was alive. Even though he was a kid in the dream, I could tell that he was happy and in a good place. I guess I'd be happy if I could be a kid forever too. So maybe he went to his own personal Heaven which was being fifteen again. Maybe he just wanted to tell me that, and that I shouldn't worry about him. I guess if I'm right about what I just said, it makes me wonder about what I'll be like when I make it up there. Maybe he and I will play basketball up in the sky for all eternity, although there are a few other things I'd rather be doing forever!

Ethan found a positive meaning for his dream. He understood what probably caused it, that is, his own inner questions about his dead brother's situation and his spending the day with his brother's son.

I'm okay

Abigail was a twenty-three-year-old woman whose brother died of cirrhosis of the liver at the age of thirty-six. She had the dream three years later.

In the dream, I was driving my car to visit a friend. The road looked familiar but I got lost. I finally pulled into her driveway but it didn't look like her house. I went inside and our family was having a party but my friend wasn't there. The inside of the house was very dark, similar to what our house used to look like. I was talking with a family member who was telling me to come with her because she wanted me to see somebody. She kept pulling at me, so I went and then I saw my brother. He had his back towards me and then he turned around. He was wearing a white-collared velvet dress suit and he had a black eye. His face was soft and mushy, like the bruises on a melon, otherwise, he looked good. I started screaming, "What are you doing here!" I was really happy. We hugged and were standing and talking and I kept saying, "What are you doing here! I miss you. How come you haven't come around?" I didn't realize that he was dead. Gradually I started to notice how black and blue he was, but he was happy and smiling and he said that he missed me too. I kept hugging him and he hugged me back. And then suddenly I realized he was supposed to be dead. I was talking to him but I wasn't saying anything. It was like mental communication, not verbal. I asked him why he was here. I kept saying, "But I thought you died. Then he gave me a strange look. I started crying really hard. He was saying that he really wasn't dead; it was all a mistake. I was confused and afraid. I thought he meant that he was buried alive. I was thinking that can't be true. Then he said, "I can't explain it to you right now; it is not a good time to talk about it, but don't worry." I wanted to ask him questions but he kept cutting me off saying everything was okay. He and I kept looking at each other. I got very sad when I knew he was really dead. We looked at each other again and then mentally he said that he was happy and safe and not to worry, that everything was okay. Then he just turned around and started walking away. I grabbed his arm and said, "You can't leave yet. I want to talk to you! You just got here! I want to spend some time with you. Just stay with me for a little while. He said he was just going outside for a minute, but he would be back to talk to me later. He walked away and I was very sad. I wasn't satisfied with talking later. I wanted it now, but I accepted it because that's what he asked for. So I shrugged my shoulders and he turned around again to walk away. As I watched him walk away he just started to fade like how smoke dissipates. I knew he wasn't really physically there, but in a way I knew he was still there spiritually and that he was going to come back because he said he would.

I felt good about the dream. I think it was his spirit that came to me in the dream because he knew I really loved him and was worried about him. He came to tell me he was safe and happy and at peace.

Many dreams seem to be responses to the dreamer's questions about the fate of the deceased. Abigail chose to ignore the more ambiguous and confusing elements in the dream and to find a meaning that satisfied her cognitive need to know that her brother was all right. Among those who dreamed of dead siblings, 33 (42%) said that the dream convinced them that their dead siblings were okay.

Promised visit

In the following dream the visit in the dream had been promised. Bea was a fifty-nine-year-old woman whose sister died of cancer at the age of sixty-two.

In the dream, I was in my bed and it was early morning. Suddenly my sister appeared standing at the foot of the bed. She looked wonderful and was smiling at me. I was astonished to see her. It had been two years since she died. She told me she just came to visit me and to tell me she was happy and that everything was going to be okay for me too. I laughed for joy and said, "You can't be a ghost because I'm talking to you." Before she left, she gave me a number to play. She and I loved to play the numbers. Then she said she had to go and smiled and slowly vanished.

When I woke up I was disappointed that she left so soon. The dream made me realize how much I missed her. Yet it also made me feel relieved, knowing that she was okay. Then I remembered. She kept her promise. When she was dying, she promised she would come back to visit me and give me a number if she could, and she did. And the number was right and I won!

Bea and her sister had been very close and talked about everything, even death and the beliefs in the afterlife. When Bea had the dream, her reactions were mixed. She felt the pain of her sister being out of her life, but was so happy for the brief visit, especially when she remembered how it had been her sister's promise to her before she died.

Warnings

Carolyn was thirty-two and dreamed of her sister who died of AIDS at the age of thirty-four. Carolyn had the dream one month after her sister died.

In the dream, I was in my bedroom asleep at night. She called me and when I opened my eyes she was sitting on the bed. I was scared because I knew she was dead. She assured me that she was okay but she had to come back and warn me to be careful or I would end up just like her. She had a serious look on her face and asked me if I understood. When I said I did, she disappeared and I woke up.

I was sweating and it felt as if she had really been in my room. I was really afraid that something was going to happen to me. I thought about how I was not being careful sexually. In fact, at that time, I was sexually involved with more that one person. The dream really scared me. I'm being a lot more careful since the dream.

The warnings vary in content. The next dream is a warning about something different. Forrest was a twenty-five-year-old man whose cousin died in a car accident when he was twenty-six. Forrest had the dream one week later.

In the dream, I was in the hospital visiting him after the auto accident. He was lying in a bed with lots of tubes in him. Suddenly, he looked up, shook his head and said he was tired. Then he coughed really bad and fell back unconscious. That was the end.

When I woke up I remembered how bad he looked in the hospital, so different from before the accident. I remembered how we would get wasted together. At the time, I was drinking a lot to get over the pain of his death. The dream was a wake-up call. I had to stop drinking so much. I had to get my act together and become more serious. The dream made me resolve not to drive anymore if I'm drunk. That's why he died. I could have died with him that night.

Messages about responsibilities

Among those who dreamed of dead siblings, 20 of them (26%) said the dream made them think about something they should do. Among those who dreamed of dead cousins, 14 subjects (28%) said the same thing.

Deaths require both personal and social adjustments in the life of the bereaved. In the next three dreams, the meanings given to the dreams are that they are messages about responsibilities they needed to assume. Dorothy was a twenty-three-year-old woman who dreamed of her brother who killed himself when he was thirty-one.

I was at school here in the United States and so I didn't get to see or talk with my brother before his death. Then, one month after he died, I had this dream. He appeared to me in my room one night. He was dressed all in white and looked peaceful. He told me he was okay and that I should not worry about him. Then he told me, that since I was the oldest, he wanted me to take care of our mother, our sister and brother. At that time I wasn't talking to my sister. He wanted me to start talking to her again. I objected but he said I was upsetting him. He told me it was really important to do it. He waited until I said, "Okay, I'll do it." and then he disappeared. The dream reminded me of my brother and how much I looked up to him. It assured me that he was okay. Most of all, it made me think about my behavior toward my sister. The dream was telling me to start accepting responsibility in the family and for my actions which included finding a way to communicate with my sister.

Here's a similar message dream about taking care of members of the family. Elizabeth was a thirty-year-old woman who dreamed of her brother three and a half months after he died from injuries sustained in an accidental fall when he was twenty-six.

> In the dream, I was walking along a street when I saw him walking towards me. I was amazed and happy to see him. We hugged and I asked him how he was. He said, "Fine. I told you I'd come back." Then he started talking about our brother and he asked me to take care of him or he said he would have to take him with him. (I didn't know that my other brother had started using drugs after the death.) Then he said he was going to visit our mother. The next day, my mother told me he visited her in a dream. A month later I had another dream. This time, I was sitting on the front porch when he came by. He wasn't alone but our dead cousin was with him. They came up and sat on the porch with me and we talked. Then my brother said, "I see you talked to our brother and that he is getting help. Thanks." That was it. Since these dreams, my belief in life after death has become much stronger.

The third dream comes from Grace, a forty-nine-year-old woman whose cousin died of cancer when he was fifty. Grace had the dream two months later.

> In the dream, I was walking along this path in what looked like a park. There were people passing by but no one that I knew. I felt someone tap me on my shoulder and when I turned around there was no one there. So I turned back around and just kept walking. A while later I felt someone tap my shoulder again. When I turned around this time, it was my cousin. He asked me to come for a walk with him because he needed to ask me something. I was shocked and scared but I figured that he was my cousin and I trusted him when he was alive so I should trust him now. He led me out of the woods and into an open field. As we walked, we discussed old times and the family. He even called me "Rags" which was his nickname for me. When we got to the end of the field he turned to me and told me that it was good to see me again but that he had a request. He made me promise to help out his wife, who was having a hard time coping with his death. I said that I would. Then he told me that I should start eating more because I looked like a stick. Then he laughed, said goodbye, and walked away. That's when I woke up.
>
> The dream made me remember a lot of good things about my cousin and how much I missed him. I started to realize what a good person he was and that I'm like him, so that makes me good too. I also thought about his wife and the rest of the family and how despite the annoying things that some of them do, I really love them all very much.

Messages of comfort

The meanings found in the next three dreams were all messages of comfort, although the first one was quite somber, for it was a message of impending death. Harriet was ninety-three years old. She dreamed of her sister nine months after her sister died at the age of ninety-two.

> In the dream, I was sitting in the living room of my house. It was a bright and sunny afternoon. Suddenly my sister walked in the room, came over to me and sat down next to me. I was astonished. She said she just came for a visit. She told me that she was fine and that Heaven was beautiful. Then she looked at me seriously and told me that I would be there with her soon. That didn't shock me, but I was surprised that she knew I had terminal cancer which had just recently been diagnosed.
>
> The dream comforted me and gave me a sense of peace. At my age, a person knows the end is coming. The dream indicates it is coming sooner because of my illness. The dream made me think of what I can look forward to, life in Heaven with my sister and the rest of my deceased family. It also told me to keep a strong faith.

Among those who dreamed of dead siblings, 28 (36%) said they found comfort in the dreams. Among those who dreamed of dead cousins, only 7 (14%) said they found comfort in the dreams.

Some religions teach that you should hope for a dream in which the dead visit. In the next dream, Khadijah used what she had learned as a Muslim to interpret her dream. Khadijah was twenty-one and her older sister was twenty when she was murdered. Khadijah had the dream two months after the death.

> In the dream, I was in my bedroom when my sister just walked in. I was astonished to see her. She stood there smiling and then she pointed to her things. She sat down and made herself comfortable and just started talking to me as if she knew she had passed away. She said, "You know now that I'm gone, you get to have all my Timberlands. You can have all my leather jackets, too. You'll be looking nice." I was crying and said, "I don't care about your stuff. I'd rather give it all away and have you here." She came over and sat next to me and said, "I'm fine. I'm okay. Look at it this way. Now you don't have to wash dishes in order to wear my sneakers or borrow my leather coat. It's there for you anytime you want. It's my gift to you." The dream sort of faded with the two of us sitting on the bed, talking.
>
> When I woke up, I felt good in part because of my Muslim belief. When someone who has been called back to Allah returns to you in a dream, I was taught that is a blessing. It's a reward from Allah allowing you to become settled. You're not worried anymore because you know the person is okay. So it made me feel good. When I first saw her in the hospital, she didn't look like my sister. She had been shot in the face. But Allah allowed her to come back and I saw that she was all right.

The message in the next dream comforts the dreamer with a promise that his dead sister would return. Gary was a fifty-year-old man who dreamed of his sister who was fifty-five when she died from cancer. The dream occurred two years later.

It was night and I was in my apartment when suddenly she appeared to me. I was so happy to see her that I jumped up and ran over to her and hugged her. We both knew she was dead and we cried as we held each other. After a while, we sat down on the couch together and talked. I told her how much I missed her and she said she knew this and that's why she came to visit. She told me I should stop crying about her being dead because she was coming back to live with me. When I asked what she meant, she just smiled and told me to be patient and in time I would know what she meant. Then she said she had to go, so we said goodbye and I woke up.

I was so happy to have seen my sister, but I was puzzled by her words. Then, nine months later, my daughter gave birth to a girl who looked just like my sister. I remembered the dream and I believe that was what she had meant. Her spirit had been reborn in my granddaughter.

Gary was a Christian, yet the meaning he found for the dream involved the belief in reincarnation!

Chapter 6: Dreams about Spouses

Some people believe marriages are made in heaven. Others think of them simply as human institutions. Many publicly declare their spousal promises to each other in a religious ritual. Others are content with a civil ceremony. This chapter offers glimpses into spousal grief through the dreams and interpretations of widows and widowers. For some, the dream led them to a new understanding of their marriage; for others it convinced them that the relationship continues beyond death. There were 66 interviews with people who dreamed of dead spouses.

The death of a spouse presents challenges to the surviving spouse. These challenges vary greatly depending on many different factors including the age of the spouses, how long they were married, the quality of the relationship, and the way he or she died. In the first example, the dreamer mourns the kind of marriage that might have been but was not.

What might have been

Isabella was sixty-two. Her husband was sixty-two when he died of cancer. She had the dream one month later.

> It's important that you know that for more than thirty years my husband suffered with chronic kidney disease. In the dream, I was on a cruise ship and I met the nicest person I've ever met. It was my husband but he was healthy, vigorous, kind and loving—all the things that were absent in reality in my marriage. As the dream ended, we were standing on the deck, face to face. He called me a "champion." Then I got off the ship, but he stayed on board. It was peaceful as he let me go and I realized the ship sailed and we went our separate ways.
>
> When I woke up, I wasn't upset or worried. It was a wonderful, sweet dream. He was okay and I was okay. The dream made me happy. I often recall the dream to reassure myself that despite unusual, difficult, and even

horrendous circumstances, I can imagine with pleasure what might have been if he hadn't been so sick. He had developed kidney disease when he was only thirty years old. From then on our life was chaotic. The dream showed me what might have been if he hadn't been so sick. He was always on drugs and they changed him. He was angry most of the time. I think of whom he might have been and wish he had been. I grieve not for his death, but for all the years that might have been if he'd have been well. In the dream he was totally different – kind, generous, and not so controlling and dependent on me. He gave me permission to live. He told me my decisions were good, that I did all I could do as a wife, a mother and a daughter. He told me I should trust my decisions and that there are loving persons to help me along the way.

I have felt his presence since the dream. I know he is watching out for me. I believe he once kept me from an accident by turning the wheel of my car. Then when my car was having more and more things go wrong, it was washed away in a flood and I received three thousand dollars for it. Finally, when I decided to sell our house, it sold for a decent price within a week. It feels so good to talk about him. I'm still grieving but nobody wants to listen.

Isabella's dream was peaceful and healing. She clearly had found a new relationship with her dead spouse. Sometimes, though, the dream is mostly painful, as in the next dream.

Guilt

Harry was a sixty-eight-year-old man who dreamed of his wife four months after she died of cancer at the age of fifty-six.

In the dream, what happened related to what had been going on in our marriage. I was playing golf, which was and is my passion, and I was planning to play on a Saturday morning. I was also asked to meet a perspective member of the golf club, and I had offered to take him around in the afternoon. So I would be playing eighteen holes in the morning and eighteen holes in the afternoon. I went to bed on Friday night and I had not dreamed of my wife since she died. But that night I did. In the dream, I can remember that all of a sudden my wife was there. I was home, in our bedroom when she walked into the room. It was so real, I was disoriented. I thought she was alive and coming to bed. Then I became confused because I knew somehow that she was not supposed to be there. My mind was racing. I was elated, thinking how great it was that she hadn't really died. She inquired about my plans for the following day. So I told her that I was playing golf in the morning, and I was going to play again in the afternoon. She looked at me very crossly, and said "Do you mean to say that you plan on playing thirty-six holes of golf and you never even had the decency to ask me if I minded?" I remember asking myself why I had done that, and realized that I had been unfair. After all, I was going to be gone all day, and I didn't even bother to ask her. I knew I had made a mistake and was about to apologize when a part of my mind took over and I realized that she hadn't really been there after all, and the reason I didn't clear my schedule with her is because she was not there. That's when I woke up.

Initially, the dream made me feel great because my wife was back, but some part of me realized she wasn't supposed to be there and yet there she was. That felt really good. But my feelings changed very much when she asked about my plans and I had to tell her I'd be playing golf all day. The fact is that when she was alive, she was always very jealous of my golf because it took up so much time. It was a bone of contention in our marriage. So in a way, the dream mirrored our marriage. There was always a bit of guilt that I experienced when I played golf. She would resent it, but I felt I was entitled to it. Nevertheless, it was always a source of friction in our marriage. I think after my wife died, I had guilt about a lot of things in our relationship, and the dream dealt with one of them. I had never dealt with any guilt about anything that occurred during our marriage while my wife was alive. After she died, all of a sudden, I was faced with things I had not dealt with before. It was painful.

Eleven of those who related their dreams about dead spouses said the dream left them with feelings of guilt. As we saw above, guilt is most common in survivors of a family member's suicide. Here's an example where the husband killed himself. Alexis was a fifty-year-old woman whose husband committed suicide when he was fifty-five. She had the dream two years after his death.

I dreamed I was sitting on the beach in front of our house where we lived before we came to America. My husband came walking along the beach. He came up to me and sat down. We started to talk about our life and his death. He told me he was at peace now and that I should not worry about him. He said he was sorry for what he had done but that everything was going to be all right. Then he got up and walked down the beach away from me.

When I woke up, I felt very bad. I recalled our marriage and thought that if I had done more to make my husband happy, then he would still be here today. I believe he died because I was not a good enough wife. I thought about all the things I should have done differently. I was surprised that the dream took place in Greece. We were very happy when we first got married and lived there. We had no problems. When we came to America, everything was hard and the problems started. I think I was worried about the wrong things and didn't pay enough attention to his needs.

Despite the message of comfort and apology from her husband, Alexis finds no comfort in the dream. It only triggered her deep feelings of guilt. The only meaning Alexis gave to the dream was that it made her realize how she had worried about the wrong things after they came to America. She would benefit from grief counseling to help her deal with the guilt.

Anger

The way someone dies really affects survivors. A tragic death of a spouse can elicit great anger, which may be suppressed but uncovered in a dream. In the following example, the death of his mother seems to have triggered the dream that revealed some raw feelings. One death will often release unfinished grief from a previous death.

Isaac was a thirty-four-year-old man whose wife was twenty-nine when she died along with her unborn son due to complications in childbirth. He had the dream two years later.

> My mother had just died and then I had the dream for the first time. I think it took place in my house. It was all foggy inside. There were people standing around but I couldn't recognize them. Then I saw my wife in the mist. She was holding our baby. She was screaming in pain and I could see that my son's face was blue and contorted. I woke up in a cold sweat, screaming, "No." I felt so much anger inside me, it scared me. I realized I was still furious at the doctors and at God. I can never forgive God for taking them both. When you really love someone you can never stop thinking about them. I know what makes it even harder for me is that I not only lost my wife but my only child as well. We were about to be a family and then nothing! It's hard to forget that. So far I have not forgotten and I don't think I ever will.

Grief following such a tragic death of not one but two loved ones is intense and takes a long time to heal. Such complicated grief usually needs intervention through grief counseling or support groups to manage the anger.[35] In the study, among the 133 accidental deaths, 49 of the dreamers (36.8%) said the dream filled them with feelings of anger.

In the next dream, anger is again uncovered in the dream, challenging the surviving spouse. Julie was a sixty-year-old woman whose husband died from cancer at the age of fifty-two. She had the dream three months later.

> I was in a church. My husband stood next to a coffin with his back to me. When he turned, all I could see was his body; I couldn't see his face. Then the dream changed and I saw him lying in the casket and again I couldn't make out his face. That was it.
>
> I woke up and the bedroom smelled of his aftershave even though the windows were closed. The dream made me realize that I was still feeling angry at him because he died and left me to fend for myself. After all those years of him taking care of me, he left me and I had to learn to survive on my own. He didn't prepare me for it, and it's been so hard. Talking about it makes me feel purged and somewhat free of the resentment that I have been feeling. I think I am beginning to forgive him for leaving me.

Julie realized forgiveness was a matter of letting go of the anger and accepting what happened and moving on by making the needed adjustments in life. Often the bereaved widows like Julie wait months and even years before they ask for the help they need to adjust to the changes in their lives.

Letting go

Kim was a forty-two-year-old woman who dreamed of her husband who died in a drowning accident when he was forty. She had a series of dreams that began with this dream.

In the dream I was in a house in the country. I knew the house but it wasn't mine. It was near a lake and I was standing at a window looking out at the beautiful scene. Then I saw my husband. He was on the other side of a wall that separated us. There was one small window and that's how I knew he was on the other side. I knew he was dead, but was so happy to see him I asked him to pass through the wall so I could hug him. He said he couldn't do that. From the expression on his face, he seemed upset with me for asking. I wanted to know what was wrong but I woke up before I could ask. The dream upset me because he seemed upset with me. It was the first dream I had about him after he died and that had been three and a half years ago. It made me wonder about the separation between the dead and the living and the limits in their ability to connect.

The second dream was a month later. In this dream, I was sitting on a park bench at the edge of a beautiful open field. It was sunny and there were beautiful flowers growing everywhere. Suddenly he was sitting on the bench with me. I hugged and kissed him and told him how much I missed him. When I asked how he was, he told me he was fine. Then he got serious and told me he couldn't stay and couldn't visit anymore. Then he disappeared. I felt sad and helpless. It made me feel like we were breaking up. It also made me think about my male friend who wanted us to become more intimate.

The third dream occurred two months later. I was sitting on the same park bench in the open field when he suddenly was sitting next to me again. He asked me how I was and I said fine. Then I asked him if he ever cheated on me. He said, "No! But you know that!" Then he looked in my eyes and said that if it would make it easier, he would say he had and then it would be easier for me to let go of him. Then he said very deliberately, "Kim, let me go." I started to cry but said, "Okay." Then he disappeared and I woke up crying. This time, however, I felt relieved. I was sad but peaceful. I wasn't upset. It was over and it was all right. Two weeks later, I felt free enough to get engaged.

There were other series of dreams that, like Kim's, reflected different degrees of adjustment in the grieving process.

For many widows and widowers, however, the dreams made them think the relationship is not over but continues. This sometimes meant that they believed the dead spouse could warn them about things for their health and happiness. Here are some examples.

Timely health warnings

Hannah was sixty-seven and dreamed of her husband two months after he died of prostate cancer at the age of seventy-two. They'd been married for forty-two years.

The dream took place while I was down South in our home in the country. It was July. In my dream I was sitting on the front porch by myself late at night snapping peas and cutting okras. All of a sudden, I felt a soft tap on my shoulder. I thought it might be one of my grandchildren wanting something, but as I turned around, I saw my husband standing there with his fishing gear and shot gun. (These were two of the things he loved to do when we went down South during the summer and winter.) He looked really good, as if he was really physically there with me. He didn't look sick like he did the last time I saw him before he died. In the dream he pulled up a crate next to me and began to talk to me about how I was doing, the kids, and family stuff as he was cleaning his gun and fishing rod. Then he began to ask me about my health. He kept saying that I didn't look so good and needed to go to the doctor and get a thorough check up. He repeatedly asked me how I felt and told me I should eat healthier food at my age, and take care of myself better than I was. I felt that this was very odd coming from a person like him. He was a firm believer in using home remedies for illnesses. He also did not believe in going to doctors, because he felt they just took your money and did not know what they were doing. He also was a man with a very healthy appetite. He never watched what he ate and was never known to be sick a day in his life. The dream ended with him getting up off the porch after having this conversation with me. He took his hunting gun and fishing rod with him, but not without telling me one more time to go to the doctor and get a thorough examination as soon as possible because I didn't look well. As he went out of the porch door into the black darkness he told me to stop being so stubborn and go make a doctor's appointment because I didn't look well. Then he told me, "Trust me. I'm doing this because I love you." Then he faded into the night.
　　The dream made me feel frightened because his whole conversation was about me needing to go to the doctor because I didn't look well. I felt the same and thought I looked the same and did not know what he was talking about. I had never been to a doctor a day in my life and never felt the need to go to one in all these years. But, since my husband kept talking about going to the doctor it made me upset. It made me think about whether what my husband was saying was true. Was I really in danger? Was I really sick? Should I go to the doctor and get examined? Could I really be sick and not know it? The dream did ease my grief, because I had been wondering when he was going to come to me and let me know that he was all right. But, I didn't expect to get a lecture on my health! It was good I got to the doctor for an examination. Maybe if my husband had gone for regular check ups, the cancer would have been detected sooner and he might still be alive. Anyway, I did what he asked me to do and found out I had very high cholesterol which made me a candidate for a heart attack. So now I'm taking medication and on a strict diet, not eating a lot of

fried and fatty foods that I used to. I feel my husband is my savior, because if I didn't go to the doctor like he advised me, I probably would not be here.

Among those who dreamed of dead spouses, 34 said the dream convinced them that the dead spouses were looking out for them, so the relationship definitely continued.

In other dreams, this was apparent because of warnings that kept the surviving spouses out of harm's way. Here's an example. Josh was a fifty-year-old man who dreamed of his wife ten years after she died from cancer at the age of thirty-seven.

> In the dream I was sleeping in my bed when my wife and my grandmother who was also dead appeared standing at the side of my bed. They both looked very serious. My wife told me that I should not leave the house the next day. She said she had something for me to do. Then she repeated that I should stay home the next day and not go to work. My grandmother was nodding her head as my wife spoke. Then she said to my wife that she should stay with me the next day. Then they both looked at me for some response, so I said, "Okay!" Then they disappeared and I woke up.
>
> I was happy to see them but worried about their message. They looked so serious when they warned me not to go to work. So I didn't set the alarm clock and slept late the next morning and missed my bus to work. I stayed home and did some work around the house. Later that day, I learned the bus had crashed and six people were killed and many others seriously injured. Now I believe my wife is watching over me. I'm convinced of it!

Messages of encouragement

Sometimes the dream comforts the dreamers because it reassures the dreamers that they are not dying. Fears are especially strong when they have the same disease as that which caused the death of the spouse. This is true in the next dream. Lauren was sixty years old and she dreamed of her husband one year after he died of pancreatic cancer at the age of sixty-three.

> In the dream I was home in bed and he came into our room and got in bed with me. I asked him why he was lying down and he groaned and said he wished he could cut off his body from the chest down. I wondered if he was alive or dead and I touched his side and it was very hard and I knew he was dead even though he seemed alive. He asked me to get him a thermos of coffee to take with him, so I went to the kitchen to prepare the coffee. When I brought it to him he was standing behind a door. (In Italian we say that your fortune awaits you behind a door.) He said he had to go. He told me not to worry, that everything was going to be all right. Then I gave him the thermos and he disappeared. It was a strange dream but I felt reassured. I felt bad to see him suffer, yet he seemed okay with leaving and going back to the nether world. I was comforted by his words to me. I knew he was referring to the diagnosis of a malignancy I had received that morning. I knew how much we had both

suffered with his cancer and how I hated to hear the word. I remembered how he suffered. When he was diagnosed, they said he only had two months to live. He suffered tremendously during that time. I would give him spring water cold from the refrigerator and it seemed to cool the fire inside him. I have apprehensions about death especially such a painful death. I hope mine will not be so painful both physically and emotionally. I am concerned for my children. They are very family oriented and feel the loss of their father very much. The dream showed me he was watching out for me and that I'll be okay.

Lauren focused on the positive message about her health in the dream and downplayed the pain her husband seemed to be suffering in the dream.

Is he saved?

Sometimes the message in the dream addressed the dreamer's fears about the dead spouse's spiritual state in the afterlife. Here's an example. Michelle was seventy-nine and told of a dream she had years ago, three months after her husband died of cancer at the age of sixty-eight.

In the dream, it was a rainy Saturday morning. We were lying in bed together and he was reading passages from the Bible. I felt so happy he was doing that. He kept reading while I listened. (I always wanted him to read the Bible with me but he never would.) After a while, he got up and made us breakfast. We sat and ate and talked about the Bible, and how he enjoyed reading it and was glad I showed him how to understand it. We went back to bed and he fell asleep and I read the Bible some more.

When I woke up, I felt peaceful, but lonely. I missed him very much. I couldn't talk to him anymore or hug him or argue with him. Sometimes I wished I could dream about him because in my dream I could see him and touch him. The dream showed me he was okay. He was with our heavenly Father and wanted me to continue to serve the Lord. It was surprising, him reading the Bible in the dream. He was not a Christian. At one time, he did everything he could to discourage me from reading the Bible and going to church. The dream was surprising and wonderful. I had wondered if his soul was truly saved and had asked God to show me a sign and he did. My prayers for him were not in vain. The dream showed me God loves us in spite of what we say or do.

Michelle had been raised an evangelical Christian and her religion was very important in her life. Her great sorrow was that her husband had resisted her attempts to bring him around. She had loved him anyway and this dream fulfilled her wishes and left her at peace.

Resolving conflicts

Sudden deaths leave many things unfinished in a relationship. Sometimes there were arguments that were never resolved. Some dreams comforted survivors by enabling them to resolve these conflicts. Here's an example. Nicole was thirty-nine years old at the time of the interview. Her husband died in an airplane crash at the age of twenty-nine.

> Before I went to bed I prayed I could have one more moment with him to get beyond the pain of separation. And I dreamed I was at his parent's house. It was like a party and I was sitting on a couch, talking with him. During the conversation we ironed out all the stupid things that had gone wrong in the relationship, a lot of immature things. There was a lot of reconciliation between us. That's what it felt like. The dream ended with us in bed, in each other's arms. It wasn't just sex; we held each other. It felt like true love. As I was holding him, he disappeared out the window and became a star in the sky and it twinkled and pulsed.
>
> I woke up feeling so much better. I remember realizing he was dead but also I recalled the happiness we had shared. I felt I faced the conflicts in our relationship and discovered true love. It felt like I had overcome a lot of obstacles. I woke up fresh, revived, and peaceful. I got past the pain, the hurt, and misunderstandings. I felt special like I had a spiritual husband to help raise our daughter born eight months before he died. The dream showed me love continues to exist after death. It never stops. The dream brought the past, the present, and the future together for me. It also made me understand that there is a child in all of us that needs to be held in order to be whole.

Nicole's dream transformed her grief. Even though it occurred only three days after he died, it brought about emotional and cognitive changes that showed her she could get on with her life and raise her daughter without him.

Unfinished business

Here's an example of a dream in which the deceased comes back to tie up loose ends with his wife. Pam was a fifty-year-old woman whose husband died suddenly of viral myocarditis at the age of thirty-three. She had the dream three months after his death.

> In the dream he came to me in our bedroom and sat down on the bed. He smiled at me and looked happy and well. He told me that God allowed him to come back on earth because there were things he needed to tell me. He told me it was just some unfinished business he needed to take care of. So he came back to tell me not to worry about him, because he was fine. He told me not to be sad, not to be unhappy, but to go on with my life, and if I fell in love again, to get married again. And he told me not to worry about anything as far his pension and life insurance was concerned, that his fellow troopers would take

care of things and they would help me over the rough months ahead. Finally, he told me not to worry about anything because he would be watching out for me. And then with that, he said he had to get back to Heaven. The dream ended with him hugging me and telling me not to worry. Then he turned and left to go back to heaven. I watched him walk to the door and disappear.

The dream left me feeling kind of sad because I was still depressed over the fact he died so young. At that time, it was only a few months after he died. I went through lot of different angry thoughts like why did I have to lose him so young, and why couldn't it have been a drug addict? He was my best friend. I was suffering a combination of anger, disbelief that he was gone and loneliness. The feelings that I had didn't come in any particular order. Different feelings came at different times. I went through periods of depression and anger. I would get into my car and drive around and cry and scream, "Why did this have to happen to me?" Then I would go through periods of panic. How was I going to survive? How was I going to raise a child alone? He died a month before my daughter's sixth birthday. She was with me when we found him and I worried how it was going to affect her. I worried if I was going to be able to manage a job and take care of her and be a good mother without him to help. My biggest fear was becoming ill myself and having something happen to me and having her left without either parent. That was my biggest fear at the time. I marveled at how real the dream was. I wondered if it was really something supernatural. I had a friend who told me to pray to my guardian angels and they would communicate with me. Was my husband really communicating with me? Is he my guardian angel? I really didn't know what to believe about it. I just thought it was strange that it happened so soon afterwards. But then I had the dream again. The thing that surprised me the most was the content of the dream. For example, there was the fact that he came to me and told me that God allowed him to come back to earth to tell me things that were left unsaid because he died so suddenly, and that he had to go back to Heaven because his work on earth was finished, and that he was just being allowed to come back and console me. The last thing he said to me was, "I love you a whole big bunch." That's what he always used to say. Hearing those words was very comforting.

Pam described the emotional roller coaster ride following her husband's death. Denial would morph into anger and then loneliness to the point of depression. This emotional process is similar to the stages described by Elizabeth Kubler-Ross.[36]

Pam also worried about the practical adjustments she needed to make to go on living without her husband. Her husband had not prepared her for this possibility. At first Pam was skeptical of the dream's spiritual reality, but after the second time, she believed it to be a message from him expressing his continued love and care for her as well as a confirmation that he was all right.

Samantha's husband also died suddenly from heart disease, but her dream was five years after the death and so there are differences. Samantha was forty-five years old when she dreamed of her husband.

I was home with a broken arm, and I was very restless. I was thinking about what I had been through the past five years. I lost my husband, my house, my car, everything in my life. I was living in a new apartment trying to put my life back together. I found myself thinking about my husband. I never had time to mourn. I wondered if he was okay. So I asked God to let me know in some way. Later that afternoon I fell asleep for about two hours, and I dreamt of my husband. In the dream he was in a house with other people, relatives and small children. I didn't actually know if they were relatives. I just sensed this. I was more interested in my husband. I ran to him and hugged and kissed him. I was so happy, knowing my honey was fine. He looked much younger than when he died. He showed me around the house and we went from room to room. Something very weird struck me. There was a refrigerator in every room we entered! There was one in the kitchen, but also they were in the dining room and living room. Christmas decorations were everywhere. Children were rushing back and forth putting decorations on trees. But it wasn't Christmas really; it was February. Adults were at the dining room table, and they all greeted me warmly, but I didn't recognize them. However, I knew my husband was okay and that made me very happy. Then something told me I didn't belong there and I told him I had to leave; he said he understood and it was all right. He said he had to get a bottle of wine for his relatives, and so we kissed goodbye and he went one way and I went the other. It was then that I noticed that we weren't walking; we were floating on air, so I made the motions of flapping wings like a bird and I called to him and said, "Look, honey, I'm flying." That's when I woke up.

I felt so happy to see him and see how happy he was. I remembered how he loved hosting parties at our house and how we had three refrigerators, one in the kitchen, one in the basement, and one in the garage! It felt so good to say goodbye to him and know he was all right. I remember that I woke up laughing. I was so relieved.

Samantha had gone through five years of painful adjusting, which included many losses. Her husband had made no provisions for his death and had only a small life insurance policy from his work. Samantha had survived and attended to all the practical details that needed attention. Five years later, she realized she still had some grieving to do. She still needed to say her final goodbyes to him. She prayed for God's help and interpreted the dream as an answer to her prayer.

More messages of comfort

Among those who dreamed of dead spouses, 24 (38%) said they were comforted by the dream. Sudden deaths, tragic deaths, such as accidental deaths, leave survivors in great need of comfort. The deaths made them very insecure. They needed to feel safe. Rebecca was forty-three years old and related a dream she had of her husband six months after he died in a car accident.

In the dream I was standing in the living room of our old apartment. My husband and I first moved there when I was pregnant with our daughter. I was walking through the place and it seemed deserted. There seemed to be fog all around and nothing was clear. I felt scared and lost. I started looking for something but I didn't know what. All of a sudden I felt a presence behind me and I turned around. My husband was standing, leaning against the wall, dressed in a white suit with a white hat on. He looked at me with his lazy smile. He lit a cigar and said "I know, I know. You don't like it when I smoke." "It's okay," I said, "do whatever you want." I was in shock. I couldn't believe he was actually there. "What are you doing here?" He replied, "What! Aren't you happy to see me? I'm happy to see you. You look great!" "Thanks," I said, "you look good too. How have you been? I've been very worried about you. I miss you." He said, "Oh, honey, don't worry about me. I'm fine. I came to tell you this." Then, he took my hand and hugged me. I started crying tears of joy and didn't know what to say. Then he said, "I can't stay but have to go now but don't worry about me. Okay? I'm happy. I'm just waiting for you. Don't forget I love you." And I said, "I love you too, honey." Then he let go of me. All of a sudden he was surrounded by this bright light and seemed to disappear before my eyes. The fog cleared up and I could feel myself at peace. When I woke up, I was disoriented at first. I didn't know where I was. Then I felt really happy when I remembered how happy he was. I actually felt at peace with myself, for the first time since his death. When I saw him smoking his cigar, I remembered how I used to nag him about it. I hated cigars and I didn't like it when he smoked them in the house. The dream also made me recall how handsome he was. I had been thinking a lot about him back then. I wanted to know if he was okay and I was really missing him. The dream was a great comfort, but it also gave me strength to go on with my life.

The dream made clear to Rebecca how she felt, i.e. "scared and lost." The dream presented a balanced view of her husband; there were the positives, like how handsome he was, and the negatives, like the cigars he loved to smoke. She believed the dream was a message that he was okay; she shouldn't worry about him. The dream freed her from that worry and enabled her to have more emotional energy to get on with her life.

The next dream comes from Larry who was married almost fifty years before his wife died. He was seventy-nine years old at the time of the interview. He started having the dream two months after his wife died at the age of seventy after a long illness.

I've had the dream more than once. It always takes place in the kitchen. The two of us are sitting at the kitchen table. It's a bright sunny morning. We would be having breakfast. This was my favorite time of the day. I can smell the coffee, the hot cereal, and the toast. In the dream my wife always says to me, "I'm okay now, so don't you worry about me." We eat together and talk about old times. Then the dream would end with us having our last cup of coffee.

The dream leaves me feeling very happy. She isn't sick anymore and she is her old cheerful self. When I wake up I also feel a little lonely. I miss her a lot. It makes me remember different parts of our forty-nine happy years together and how much I still love her. In a way, the dream is as if she is still with me. I love to talk about my wife. It makes me feel good, but I do miss her.

The last dream of this chapter came from Sarah, an eighty-six-year-old woman who was forty years old when her husband died of a heart attack. She had the dream one month after he died, but remembered it vividly for more than forty years.

In the dream, I was in our bedroom. I was crying and feeling so alone. Then I heard someone coming up the stairs. I recognized the sound of his shuffling steps. I also heard his voice. He was talking to someone. I sat up. I was a little afraid but also was excited that it might be him. He came into the room and stood in the doorway and smiled. I put out my arms and he came to me and hugged me. He told me he came to keep me company because he knew how lonely I was. He said he was fine and was worried about me. I asked who I heard him talking to when he was coming up the stairs. He told me it was his mother (who died two years before him); she was with him. I asked him where she was and he said she was waiting for him downstairs in the kitchen. I never saw her but heard her voice. We talked some more and he promised he'd be watching over me. Then we said goodbye and he left.

I was so happy to see him. I realized he would always be with me. I felt protected, that he was always watching over me; I've never felt alone and still feel that way today.

Many dreams in the study seemed to have had lasting effects on the dreamer. Sarah's interview offered evidence that the effects could last a lifetime.

Chapter 7: Dreams about Children

The loss of a child is one of the most painful deaths someone can suffer. Even if the child is an adult, it is still very difficult for the parents. Such a death seems out of order; children should outlive their parents. The death of a child robs a parent of biological immortality, of living on in their offspring. It steals the dreams and hopes parents have for their children.[37] Here are some dreams from mothers and fathers who suffered such losses. There were only 34 cases in the study, but they were good examples of the different faces of grief. The chapter is arranged according to the age of the son or daughter, beginning with the youngest.

A miscarriage

Ashley was forty-four years old at the time of the interview. Seven years earlier, she had suffered a miscarriage. One week later, she had a dream.

> The dream began with me walking down the middle aisle of the church I attended when I was in elementary school. I was holding the baby in my arms. He was dressed in a little white robe. He looked like an angel. I was wearing a long black dress and as I neared the front pews I felt colder and colder. When I finally reached the altar, there was a priest there who had baptized my two other children. He had died since then. He was standing there with my deceased parents. They were all smiling at me. I brought my baby up to the priest and he blessed the baby and poured holy water over his head. Suddenly the baby disappeared from my arms. That's when I woke up.
>
> The dream left me feeling peaceful. It made me think that my son would be in good hands. My parents would be there to take care of him. The dream also relieved me of some guilt I had that I had somehow caused the miscarriage.

Guilt is common after miscarriages, but Ashley's guilt was relieved by the accepting attitude of the priest and her parents. Her wishes to know her baby was all right were also satisfied. Thus the dream was a balm for Ashley's painful emotions and thoughts. Among those who dreamed of dead offspring, 23 (67%) said the dream made them believe the deceased was okay, and 22 of them (64%) said they were comforted by the dream.

Babies

Bertha had feelings of self-doubt after her son died from SIDS. She was thirty-eight years old when she told the story of how her son died when he was six months old. The dream occurred three months after the death.

> I saw my baby and he looked healthy. He was in the arms of my father who was also dead. The place appeared to be Heaven because everything was bright and white, and there was a great sense of peace in the dream. Then I saw Jesus and he took my father and my baby up into a cloud.
>
> When I woke up, I felt comforted and relieved, knowing that my son was fine and everything was okay. I had been depressed after his death and doubted how good a mother I was. The dream gave me a sense of well-being as far as my parenting. This was important because I have four other children. The dream also took away my fear of any of my other children dying because now I know where they are going. It also made me think about the second coming of Jesus and how those who are saved will go with Jesus to Heaven.

Bertha's self-doubts about being a good mother were relieved by the dream. She had been raised a Baptist and she related how important her religion was to her. The fact that the dream images confirmed what she had been taught about the afterlife was very comforting. It also motivated her to be an even better Christian.

The baby in the next dream also died when he was six months of age. Carolyn was forty-nine at the time of the interview. Her son died from kidney failure. She had the dream three years later.

> In the dream, I had just died and was walking on a beautiful road with all kinds of flowers on each side. The further I walked, the more the road seemed to open up for me. As I approached a turn, there stood a little boy who looked to be about three years old. He looked like my son would have looked. I remember the dream as if it was yesterday. The boy said to me, "Come, Mama, it's time to go home." (I deeply believe "home" meant Heaven.) He reached out his hand to take mine and I started to cry and I woke myself up.
>
> The dream made me feel elated. I really thought I was on the road to the Kingdom of Heaven. The dream showed me my son was in a good place. It also explained why he had to die. The dream showed me that he had become our family's guardian angel. Finally, the dream revealed God's love for me, for he showed me my son in Heaven.

Carolyn, like Bertha, understood her dream in the context of the religious beliefs she had been taught. She found the answer for why her son had to die so young, as well as confirmation of God's love for her.

Young children

Donna was forty-nine years old. She vividly remembered a dream she had fifteen years earlier of her three-and-a-half-year-old son. He had died six months earlier as the result of a tragic accident.

> The dream took place somewhere like in a daycare center or a big playroom. The place had a lot of toys and many children involved in different activities. The children all seemed very happy and all of them were dressed in clean pretty white outfits and seemed very much at home in their surroundings. My son ran over to me and told me, "Mommy, don't cry. I love you. Mommy, I forgive you. I'm okay, so don't worry about me because I have lots of friends and toys here." Then he ran off with other children and started to play. At that point the lady that was there with the children gave me a hug and told me not to worry about him because he is safe. Then she escorted me to a door and told me not to worry, that everything was going to be all right. Then I woke up.
>
> The dream left me feeling very relieved because I blamed myself a great deal for what happened to my son. By having the dream, I felt that he was able to forgive me although I knew I was not a good mother to him. My son died after falling from a fifth floor window because I was not properly supervising him because of my serious drug addiction. The dream made me think about my son a great deal. I wondered what he would have looked like or been if he had lived. If I had not been on drugs, he would have been right here with me enjoying life. The dream reassured me that he did not carry a grudge against me. He had room in his heart to forgive me. This dream motivated me to turn my life around and not let drugs control my life anymore. I have been an active born-again Christian in the Baptist Church since 1984 and help educate young mothers and drug-addicted women who are trying to make positive changes in their lives. The dream changed my life.

Many dreams in the study precipitated changes in the dreamers. Some, like Donna, made dramatic changes in their lives. Like Donna's transformation, these changes were partly spiritual.

The next dream came from Justin, a twenty-five-year-old man who recalled a dream he had of his daughter who died of cancer at the age of four. The father had the dream one month later.

> It was so real. She was on the floor of the living room, playing with her toys. She stopped and looked at me and said, "Daddy, I love you." She always used to say that to me; then she went back to playing. After a while she got up, walked over to me, and kissed me on the cheek and said, "I take care of daddy." She never said that to me before. It was so surprising, I woke up.

The dream made me very happy. It was so good to see and hear her again. Remembering the kiss she gave me in the dream still brings tears to my eyes. I miss her a great deal. We did everything together. I go to the cemetery every week and talk to her. She battled cancer for eighteen months. I know she is not suffering anymore, and that's good. I understood her words to mean that she will always be with me. The dream tells me not to worry about her; she is fine. But I still miss her a lot.

This is a comforting dream for Justin, but the loss of his daughter is still fresh and there is still much sadness left inside him.

Teenagers

Heather was a thirty-two-year-old woman whose sixteen-year-old son committed suicide. She started to have the dream two weeks after the funeral.

In the dream, he is always standing in the doorway of my bedroom. He has a smile on his face and he always tells me, "Mom, I'm okay." The dream ends with him turning and walking away.

When I wake up, I always feel comforted. I am happy that he is alright. The dream reminds me about the good and not so good times we had together. My son seemed to have gotten his life together. He was going to school and making good grades, but then he took his life! I don't feel sad as much as I did when he died. I still love him very much. It would be so good to have him alive in my life, but I realize there are many people like me. Their loved ones died and they are very sad. But the dead are okay and life must go on for the living. It really helps me to talk about my son.

Heather's dream was repeated over many months. They gave her comfort in regard to the state of her son after he died. She was well along in the grieving process when she was interviewed. She had gotten beyond anger and guilt. The sadness was diminishing. One of the things she said helped her was joining a support group for survivors of suicide. It was there she realized "there are many people like me."

Jennifer was seventy-one years old when she recalled the dream she had three months after her eighteen-year-old daughter died in a car accident.

I remember the dream vividly. I was attending Mass in my parish church and at the end of Mass I saw her with Jesus and her deceased grandparents standing behind her. They were up front by the altar. I was walking out of church when I saw them. She waved goodbye to me and I waved goodbye back to her.

When I woke up, I was crying, but I felt good knowing she was safe in Heaven with the Lord and her grandparents. The dream still left me with the stabbing question of why did this tragedy have to happen. For the first three months after she died, I was really upset and angry about her death. Why did God take away a beautiful, caring, and intelligent young woman from us? She was looking forward to completing college and going on to law school. Now she would not fulfill her goals and dreams and our family would not be able to celebrate her accomplishments. The dream helped me adjust to life without her. It showed me that she was in a good place. The fact that I waved back goodbye to her showed me that I was beginning to accept that she was really gone.

Jennifer's dream helped her move toward accepting the reality of her daughter's death. It was made easier by the fact that she believed the dream indicated her daughter was in a "good place." She was still left with the gnawing question concerning why it had to happen.

Young adults

Kendra was fifty-six and recalled her dream of her daughter that she had seven months after her daughter died of viral myocarditis at the age of twenty-four. First she gives some background information.

My daughter had a virus and went to a doctor. He gave her antibiotics. Within two days she was much, much worse. She was having trouble breathing and I called the doctor and he told me to bring her to the hospital. She went to the bathroom and passed out on the floor. So I called an ambulance. We got there and I signed her into the hospital. It was ten o'clock at night. Twenty minutes later, she went into cardiac arrest and just never came back. They'd get her going and she'd code again. So at two o'clock she was pronounced dead. Seven months later, my son was getting married and a couple days before the church service, I had this dream.

In my dream I saw my daughter taking pictures of my son and my daughter-in-law. She loved to take pictures. She positioned the two of them together, and she was jumping around and taking pictures. There was no talking in the dream, but here's something strange. I had not seen the dress my daughter-in-law was going to wear, but because of the dream I could have described it to the point where it had a little sash, and one side of the bow kept slipping and one of the ribbons would hang below her hem. The dream was that clear. Also there was something about the restaurant where they had their reception. I had been in this place a couple of months before the wedding and there was a partition between the restaurant side and the bar side, but there were openings on the top. In my dream, there were blinds on these openings, which I found out later the owner put up the night before the wedding. So I had never seen them except in the dream.

To me, the dream meant she approved of the marriage. She had never met the girl that my son married, but the dream meant she approved of her. It was like she gave her blessing. The dream filled me with happiness that she was still connected to the family. The dream was very vivid. I remembered it clearly. I don't usually remember my dreams at all. I mean I get a little snippet here or there, but this, I remembered the whole thing.

I really haven't thought about this dream in a while. Her father, my husband, was also in the dream. He had a very hard time dealing with her death. In the dream, I saw her give him a long hug. I think the dream was also her way of letting me know she was going to comfort her father.

I made my peace with God the day she died. Not that I didn't grieve, but basically I made my peace with God. This was His decision. Let me explain. When they brought my daughter up to the Intensive Care Unit, I was praying for Him to take care of her. I didn't say, "Save her." I remember I never ever said, "Save her." I said, "You take care of her." And I was standing up against the wall outside of the Intensive Care Unit and I felt a hand on my shoulder. I turned and there wasn't anybody there; there was a wall there. And then I heard a voice. It said, "She's safe with me now." And I looked at the clock it was two o'clock. And when I saw the death certificate a couple days later, it said she died at exactly two o'clock. When I heard the voice, I knew it was inside my head; no one else heard it. I knew it was just me. I had such a feeling of comfort and peace. I can't really explain it to anyone. But that's how I felt and I made my peace then. So how her death affected the rest of my family was of prime importance to me. And I think that's what the dream was about. She came and she told me my son was marrying the right girl and that she would look after her father. I made my peace, but sometimes it's still difficult to talk about, even now. And then other times I don't have a problem. Everyone needs someone to talk to when they go through something like this.

Kendra revealed a lot about her grief and how her spirituality was such an important support for her. It enabled her to let her daughter go when she died. The meaning she found in the dream was comforting. Her daughter was still part of the family, and she would take care of her father whose grief was still intense. Researchers report that parents are better able to cope with the death of their child if they find a way to continue the relationship.[38]

The next dream is very different. Eric, the father, finds no peace after his son's death. Eric was forty-eight years old and told of the dream he had of his son one year after he died. He was twenty-six when he shot himself in the head.

He was the oldest of my three children. I had this dream maybe a year after the incident. In the dream, my three children, including him, and I were in a park and we were having fun. I was teaching my daughter how to ride her bike. My younger son was playing a game with other little kids in the park. When I looked around, my oldest son was nowhere to be found. So I went looking for him. I walked toward the public bathroom, and as I got near I heard noises. I heard a voice of a little girl saying, "Stop! Get off of me!" I was alarmed because it sounded like my little girl. When I walked in I saw my oldest son on top of my daughter. I don't know what happened next, but a gun flew in my hand and I shot him in the heart and my daughter ran to me crying.

When I woke up, I was shaking with rage. I was very angry and upset. Maybe if my son hadn't killed himself, I probably would have done it. He caused so many problems. The dream reminded me of how much of a pervert he was and I wondered how any child of mine could do that to anyone else, especially his own sister. I think the world is better off without him. Even though I was not the one that killed him in real life, the dream seemed so real that it really made me think that I pulled the trigger. Even though it was a dream, it opened my eyes to the fact that it was true all these years what people had been saying about him. He was a child molester. I started to have the dream when my daughter came to me and told me that she had been sexually molested for many years by him. I don't feel that I did anything wrong as a parent. I was there for my kids and I did the best that any father could have done. I wish I would have known what was going on so I could have put an end to the whole thing and probably gotten him some help. I appreciate this interview because I had a chance to talk about things that have been bothering me, a chance to clear up some unfinished business. It's been three years since the death of my older son and I still resent him. I am unable to let go of the pain. It turned out that he sexually molested my younger son as well as some other children in the area. It's going to take a lot longer than a few years to get over the shock and disappointment. I never spoke to anyone about this dream before. I feel greatly relieved.

Eric revealed many aspects of grief that follow a suicide. He was filled with anger, not because his older son killed himself but because of what he did to his siblings and other children. Eric also had self-doubts and guilt. What should he have done that he hadn't? There was also the shame of being the father of someone who molested children. The shame made it difficult for Eric to express his grief and get help managing it.

Adult children

Lisa was sixty-one years old when she recalled the dream she had of her son who died of cancer at the age of thirty-five.

In the dream, I was sitting in my friend's living room and my son was sitting next to me. I was crying and he was trying to comfort me, telling me that everything was okay. He told me that I did not have to worry about him. At that point, he got close to me and tried to hug me. When this happened, I woke up crying.

The dream made me feel very sad. I missed him so much. The dream made me realize I had to accept that my son was not here any more. I had to accept that my son was gone. He wasn't coming back. It didn't matter how much I loved him. His time was up. I had no choice but to accept it and let him go. The dream also made me believe that he was okay and looking out for me.

Lisa's dream interview was a good example of a mother's coming to accept her grown son's death. She was still full of sadness, but cognitively she accepted that "his time was up." The dream comforted her with the beliefs that he was all right and watching over her.

The next example is similar. Megan was sixty-two years old when she recalled the dream she had two and a half years after her thirty-seven-year-old, oldest son died suddenly from a stroke.

I was applying makeup to my face in the upstairs bathroom in preparation for my middle son's wedding. Downstairs, I heard a number of voices. I heard my husband, my middle son and his bride to be, my youngest son and his wife, and my oldest son, the best man. I realized, in the dream, we were all together, the whole family, for the wedding. They were laughing and having a wonderful time. I hurried to join them but woke up before I got down the stairs.

The dream was so vivid, it almost seemed real. The dream left me feeling sad; I longed for the days when no one from my family was missing. At the time of the dream, I was still grieving my son's death. The dream reminded me of the joy of that day. My middle son's wedding day was one of my happiest memories. The dream revealed to me that there would be happy days ahead, for although my oldest son could not be with us physically, he would live on in our memories and in our hearts.

Megan's sadness was great. The dream reminded her of a happy time when her eldest son was very much part of the family and it showed her how he could remain part of the family. Recalling memories of him would be the way to keep her son alive and part of the family. This realization did much to alleviate her grief.

In the last dream in this chapter, a message about Heaven confirms the faith that enabled this mother to accept her daughter's death. Nuala was a seventy-nine-year-old woman whose daughter died of cancer at the age of forty-six. The dream occurred two years after she died.

In the dream, it was late evening and I had gone to bed. I was asleep in my bed when her voice, calling me softly, woke me up. I opened my eyes and saw her. She looked radiant. We hugged and cried together. I asked her how she was and she told me that although she missed me, she was very happy in Heaven. She went on to tell me how wonderful it is but I can't remember exactly what she said. I do remember she told me to keep praying everyday. Then she kissed me and I woke up.

The dream was so real, it surprised me. It left me feeling very happy and comforted. I was excited for her. I knew she was happy and watching over me, and that we were still very close. It also made me think about Heaven, what I'd been taught we have to look forward to. The dream convinced me that my beliefs about my daughter in Heaven are right and real.

For many dreamers in this chapter, like Nuala, the inherited religious beliefs were an important part of the grieving process. For some, images of these beliefs showed up in their dreams. It was the confirmation of these beliefs that comforted the bereaved. For others, it was the simple belief that a real connection existed between the living and the dead that gave them strength to carry on.

Chapter 8: Dreams about Friends

Unlike family relationships, friends are chosen. We choose friends because we sense, consciously or unconsciously, they are good for us. One idea about friendship is that we pick people who are like us and that's why we like them. Friends are important for our self esteem because they validate who we are. We are not alone in thinking and feeling the way we do; our friends do too. In addition, with our mobile and fragmented families, friends often function as family members, often like siblings. So when a friend dies, it affects us deeply. Through dreams about dead friends, we become aware of the extent of our grief as well as having other insights about ourselves. There were 139 interviews of people who had dreams about dead friends.

Fears about death

Sandra was twenty-three years old and had this dream about a high school friend who died at eighteen when his speeding car went out of control and his car flipped over. She dreamed of him the night after his death.

> I was having a really hard time falling sleep. When I finally did, I fell asleep with one arm over my head dangling down between the end of my bed and the wall. In my dream, he was below me and he was pulling me down. I couldn't see his face, but I knew it was him. I was screaming for him to let go, but he kept pulling me down.
>
> I woke up screaming and was very upset. I was sweating and breathing very fast. I was petrified and confused. Why would he be pulling me down? It was really frightening. The dream made me think about how very scary death was to me. The dream showed me how much turmoil I was going through. I was so scared about what had happened, scared about what I couldn't understand, scared about all the things I had to face, like going to the wake and funeral. I had been thinking a lot about the fact that he would be buried under the ground. That scared me a lot. I think the dream meant I was being pulled down into the grave with him.

I was very confused about where he was since he died. I was agnostic, but knew about my friends' beliefs in Heaven and Hell. I had a lot of anxiety over what comes after death. The dream showed me how many death issues I needed to handle better. I guess the most important thing was that it made me see just how scared I was of death and what happens to someone after they die. I'm not accustomed to discussing such an issue out in the open, but I feel relieved having gotten it off my chest.

The dream offered Sandra an opportunity to confront all her fears and questions about death. Growing up in a family of agnostics, Sandra never had a chance before the death and dream to explore different beliefs about the afterlife or the reasons for different customs, like wakes and earth burial. Such opportunities would have at least given her knowledge of the options she had. Among those who dreamed of dead friends, 53 (38%) said the dream made them feel frightened.

Anger and guilt

Among those who dreamed of dead friends, 17 of the dead were murdered. Tammy was thirty-four years old and her best friend and her friend's two-year-old daughter were murdered. She had the dream six months later.

I dreamed I was at the funeral in Jamaica. It was at my friend's childhood home. I went over to the two gravesites where the caskets were and I saw my friend sitting on top of her casket. She was dressed in a beautiful sky blue dress. I ran over to her and told her how happy I was that she was not dead. She smiled and said, "Of course I'm not dead. I was only sleeping." I asked for her daughter and she turned and pointed to the other casket where I saw her daughter lying in a beautiful white dress. My friend told me that she was also sleeping. I was very anxious to know what happened and she told me that her husband drugged them and then set the apartment on fire to cover his tracks. I started to tell her to go to the police with me, but she only smiled and shook her head and told me that the Lord will deal with her husband. Then I tried to give her a hug, but woke up.

At first I was disoriented because I couldn't believe it was only a dream. It was so real. I felt very happy to have seen her. Then I felt bad as I realized what I had seen was not real. The dream convinced me that her husband was guilty and I was very angry that he was not charged with murder. He had gotten away with it. The dream made me think about a lot of things. I wondered where the soul of my friend and her daughter were and hoped they were with Jesus. I thought how fragile life was. I wondered what my friend thought about when she realized she was facing death. It bothered me that she could smile and forgive that jerk. At the time of the dream I was feeling angry and frustrated about the investigation into their deaths. The dream told me I was right not to trust my friend's husband and to trust my instincts and intuition. The last time I saw my friend and her daughter, her husband had just moved out of the apartment and left her with no money and a notice of eviction for non-payment of rent. He had lied to my friend about all the time he was working when he actually had been fired for weeks. He had not been paying the rent and other bills. I had felt uneasy and had told my friend not to let him in the apartment when she was alone and to have the locks changed until she moved out. When I learned that she and her daughter were dead, I immediately suspected him because I knew he could be ruthless and was capable of murder. I am still angry with him and with myself for not trying harder to protect my dear friend and her sweet little baby. I knew my friend would probably let him in the house. She was naive and too trusting. I should have been more forceful.

Tammy's dream revealed to her the great angry element in her grief. The anger is directed at her girlfriend's husband whom she suspected and the dream confirmed that he killed them. She is angry that he seems to be getting away with it. The dream also uncovers her guilt that she didn't do more to protect her friend and child. These two emotions dominate this dream. Tammy's is a difficult grief because of the way her friend and daughter died.

What really happened?

Among those who dreamed of dead friends, 49 of the friends (35%) died because of accidental causes, and 58 (41.7%) said the dream caused them to wonder about how the deceased died.

Angela was a twenty-three-year-old woman whose boyfriend died when he was driving home from work and was hit by a drunk driver. It's a dream she's had more than once, the first time six months after he died.

> I dreamed about the crash. It started when he left the office, got into his car and started to drive. He was on the highway when a big black and red eighteen-wheeler truck came out of nowhere and ran over his car. It didn't hit the car, it ran over it and kept going. His car was gone. Nothing was there! Nothing at all! He was lying in the middle of the road, all bloody and torn up. He was dead. In some dreams, he sat up and rubbed his head for a second and then died. That's how it ends.
>
> The dreams made me imagine what the accident was like. I believed deep down inside me that it was awful, that he probably suffered a lot. Maybe that's why I had the dream because he knew, or I knew, that that would really worry me. It did bother me. I didn't know what happened. The paramedics said he held on for about an hour, but he died before I got there. In one version of the dream, he was lying on the road but he sat up and said something like, "It doesn't feel as bad as it looks, honey." He called me "honey." As time went by, the dreams got less and less gross and creepy. They actually sort of made me feel a little bit relieved because I think they made me feel like I knew exactly what happened. I mean, I knew that's not what really happened, but it made me feel better. The truck thing used to bother me because it wasn't a truck that hit him. It was a stupid little Japanese car. I'm not so angry anymore. I was for a long time, but sometimes things happen and you just can't control

them. Life isn't fair. I miss him. I wish he were still alive, but I know he's gone. I guess that's why I don't really mind the dream anymore; it's sort of all I have left of him.

Angela's dreams, over the course of almost two years, helped her work through her grief. Her imagination, at work in the dream, led her to accept the way he died. The dream met her need to understand what happened. In the end, she realized her grief was not uncommon. Tragic deaths, like his, happen too often. She came to understand the unfairness of life.

Moving toward acceptance

The next two dreams came from Courtney, a twenty-seven-year-old woman whose best friend was murdered at the age of twenty-two. She had the first dream two weeks after the death.

> The dream took place outside the parish church. We were sitting together on the brick wall there. It's an old hangout we referred to as "the wall." I was surprised she was there because I knew she was dead. I never got to say anything to her. There was something else that was strange. I couldn't make out her face. It was all blurry. It was a very short dream but very real.
> The dream left me feeling "spooked" and upset. I really felt guilty for not warning her to stay away from her boyfriend, the guy who murdered her. The dream made me remember how brutally she died and how I didn't want to remember the way my friend's face looked at the wake. But the dream also got me thinking about someday when we will be together again in the next life.
> I had another dream about her recently. In that dream, we were at a party with a large group of our friends. What was great about this dream was that my friend's face was clear and the way I remembered her before she was murdered. I guess it means I'm accepting her death better. I really like talking about my friend.

Courtney recognized how the dreams were expressions of where she was in the grieving process, as she moved to acceptance of her friend's death. Part of the process was moving her friend out of this world into the next, with the hope of being reunited with her after her own death. This fulfills the need to find a way for the relationship not to be completely over but to continue in some way. Here's another example.

Changing the relationship

Danielle, a forty-three-year-old woman, recalled a dream she had after her friend died when they were in high school. They were both seventeen.

In the dream, I was standing near a diner where we all used to hang out and I saw a group of my friends standing over in the corner and they were all crying and hugging each other. When I walked over and asked them what they were crying about, they said that Linda had died. I remember thinking to myself I already knew that and I couldn't understand why they were in the corner crying as if it had just happened. Then all of a sudden I wasn't in the diner anymore, and I was walking up my street which is the street Linda used to live on. I wasn't really thinking about going up to her house like I used to; I was just aimlessly walking up the street. All of a sudden, she came around the corner and I stopped. I said to her, "Linda, what are you doing here?" And she started to laugh and told me she was coming down to my house to see me. I said, "But you died. What are you doing here?" She said, "No. I didn't die. It wasn't me; it was my twin sister. You know how my mom always lied. She lied and I really had a sister and it was my twin that died not me." So then we just started walking down the street together the same as we always used to. I was relieved to think she was still alive and I remember thinking in my head in the dream how that's just like Linda. She always did stuff like that. She would pull pranks on us. One time, she called my house and she was crying, and asked me to hurry over to her house. She told me she had broken her leg and was in a cast and couldn't go anywhere. So I went running up the street and I walked in her room and there was nothing wrong with her. She was just being punished and couldn't go out. She started laughing. So it seemed as if it were just another prank she was playing and the prank was over and she was still alive. While I was dreaming, I was thinking she had pulled this prank and I laughed to myself and thought, "Well isn't that just like her."

When I woke up, I wished the dream had been true and I was sad and disappointed that it was just a dream. It seemed so real. I can tell you the names of every friend who was in the diner. I had the dream a few months after her death and her death was beginning to hit me. I had been very shocked when she died. I had spent a great deal of time up at her house for two months after she died. I used to go up there and do her grandmother's hair and wash her mother's dishes and hang out in her bedroom as if she were still there. And her family let me and even liked me there. Then, all of a sudden, I realized that what I was doing was unhealthy. That sitting in her bedroom by myself listening to her CD's wasn't going to bring Linda back. I decided I had to let go so I stopped hanging out there like I was doing everyday. I realized she really was gone, but I still didn't like it. So, I think it was after that that I had the dream. I think what happened was I realized she really was dead, but the dream told me she was still with me in a different way. The dream actually made me feel close to her again. In the dream I felt she sought me out to tell me she was still alive. It was her way of letting me know that she is still around and watching.

This was an insightful reflection many years after the dream. Danielle recognized the grieving process, the two months hanging out in her friend's old room. She realized she needed to do this for her grief and Linda's family respected her needs. Grief is not rational. Bereaved people often feel the need to do things that make no sense. If their needs are respected, (providing their actions bring no harm to themselves or others) the process will continue and they won't get stuck. After two months, Danielle was ready to move on. Her interpretation of her dream helped her come to a fuller acceptance of her friend's death by transforming the relationship into a spiritual one.

The need to forgive

The next dream reveals a character fault in the dreamer. Janet was twenty-four at the time of the interview. She dreamed of a childhood friend who was hit by a car at the age of eight. The dreamer had the dream thirteen years later.

> I dreamed I was asleep in my room, but I woke up when I heard someone clear his throat. I was astonished to see that it was my childhood friend who had died thirteen years ago. He looked the same as he did before the accident. He told me he came back to apologize to me for the fight he had with me on the day he died. My memory jumped back to that day and I remembered exactly what he had done. So he is standing there waiting for my response. He apologized again. I was not feeling very forgiving and told him I did not accept his apology. He persisted in apologizing and his persistence annoyed me. Finally, I folded my arms, raised my voice and said, "No! I will not forgive you! Now go away." He looked really crushed and turned to leave. That's when I woke up.
>
> The dream really bothered me. I didn't understand why after all these years he would come back to apologize. But most of all, I felt really bad about my behavior. I thought I was a forgiving person and I was astonished to see that I would not forgive my childhood friend. We were only kids back then. Later, I thought about how, at the time of the dream, I was having a lot of conflicts with my parents and friends. I realized the dream pointed out something I do that I don't like about myself and that I want to change. The dream made me realize that I should be more forgiving and not hold onto grudges.

This is a good example of an insightful dream. Janet is confronted with her stubbornness in not forgiving but holding onto the memories of how people offended her. The dream, with her childhood friend shocks her into seeing something that she had successfully ignored. The pain of this image is enough to motivate her to change.

I'm going to Hell

Here's another insightful dream. Shirley was twenty years old and dreamed of her friend who hung himself when he was fifteen. She had the dream two months later.

> In the dream I was in a church for his funeral. He was wearing what he really was buried in. Suddenly he sat up, climbed out of the casket and walked over to me. He sat down next to me in the pew and held my hand. Then he looked in my eyes. I saw this great sadness. He said, "I miss you. Come with

me." I told him I wasn't ready to go and was staying here. He said, "I'm lonely. If I go, I'll go to Hell because I killed myself." I told him, "But God loves everyone. He'll forgive you." Then he just disappeared and I woke up crying.

It was very scary and sad. I thought of how he died and what I'd been taught in religious classes about killing yourself. Sometimes I get really depressed and even think I'd be better off dead. The dream tells me I won't be better off if I do commit suicide. It also made me think that I should study to become a psychologist to help people like my friend.

Shirley's dream caused her to reflect on her own suicidal thoughts and recall what she had learned about God's punishment of those who commit suicide. She discovers this is a good deterrent for her. It also motivated her to think about her career choice.

Dreams that changed lives

Here are two dreams which the dreamers believe transformed their awareness and their lives. The first dream came from Lou, a thirty-two-year-old man who dreamed of an older coworker and friend who died at age eighty-three. The dream occurred three months later.

He died of cancer of the pancreas. He was old. He was little. He was skinny, but he was healthy. We were really good friends for years. Then, one day, he found out he had cancer. I mean, he was going to the doctor and he was fine. That afternoon he came to the loft. Someone told me he was outside. I went out to see him. He was always sun tanned, but that afternoon he looked gray. The doctor told him he had cancer and he looked like he had aged a million years. For years, I used to kid him that he was like a million-year-old man. He liked it when I said that. Two weeks after he went to the doctor, he died. I think he just gave up. During those two weeks, I couldn't reach him by phone, and I couldn't visit to talk to him. I think he just wanted to die alone. I didn't like that and was angry at him. Then I had this dream. You need to understand that I know when I'm dreaming. I know when I'm not. I'm never really confused about the fact that I'm dreaming. Anyway, in the dream the doorbell rang and it woke me up. I got out of bed and went upstairs. I could see that it was a beautiful morning. There was no indication that I was dreaming. I thought I was totally awake. I got to the door and opened the door and there he was, standing there. Immediately I knew I was dreaming because I knew he was dead. He was standing there and tried to say something to me. I saw his lips were moving, but I couldn't hear what he said. And he was crying. I reached out to invite him to come in, but he just turned around and everything turned white, completely white, where I was standing and everywhere else. Then, I woke up.

It was weird that it didn't really seem like a dream until I saw him and by that time he mouthed a few words and split. After I woke up, I just sat up and thought about him. I thought about how he didn't even have time to die. He just found out he was sick, and then he died. Most people don't find out they have cancer and then die two weeks later. He didn't even have time to die. He was fine. He was picking me up the day before. He never weighed much, maybe eighty pounds, this little old Maltan guy. He was from Malta and that's what I called him. He liked that. Maybe he knew that I was angry at him and he realized that I was right and came to apologize. It was like he was asking me not to be mad at him, but I couldn't hear him. I think he thought I could, but I couldn't. I was sad and a little disappointed that I couldn't understand him.

The dream got me thinking about my beliefs. Before the dream I was definitely agnostic. Even though I was raised a Catholic I couldn't grasp the idea of just having faith. You know what I mean? Just have faith. So many things just didn't make a lot of sense. It wasn't the fact that my friend came to me in a dream or anything, but I think for some reason, I just suddenly knew there was a God. It wasn't even like I believed. I knew it was a fact. You could call it whatever you want, but God is a fact. It really didn't make me want to be good, per se, but it made me think that if there's a God, then there's a reason for everything, to some extent. So, I started cleaning up my act, not to the extent of Granola and a ten-mile run everyday, but just not going out all the time and drinking. I started taking care of myself, my body, my head, trying to stay somewhat sane. The dream made me aware that I was destined for something. There was a reason, not necessarily a mission, for me to be here. It's not that concrete. I don't think I'm here to save your life tonight. It's not like that. It just made me start to explore things more. I was aware that there was a place for me, and I just started trying to find out where that was.

Lou's dream uncovered something deep and spiritual in him. The dream clearly changed him in his thinking and behavior. It wasn't so much his friend's death that did it as the experience of the dream. It was so personally powerful.

The next dream came from Kayla, a twenty-one-year-old woman whose boyfriend was shot to death when they were both seventeen. She had the dream one week later.

The dream was like what really happened but with some differences. In the dream, we had gone to the movies and when we came out, we ran into friends who were waiting to go in and see the next show. We hung around, talking with them for a while. I was out of cigarettes, so I went into the store next door to buy some. While I was in the store, a black car with all black-tinted windows pulled up outside the movie theater. As it slowly passed, the windows opened and guns fired. Then it sped away. I ran out and saw my boyfriend lying face down on the sidewalk. I ran to him and knelt down next to him. He was unconscious and bleeding. When I turned him over and lifted him into my arms, he disappeared. All that was left was a pool of blood. I screamed and woke myself up.

I felt like my body was on fire and I couldn't breathe. I was shaking with terror. The dream made me realize that I could have been killed too. The dream was a wake-up call. It told me that I had a chance to change the way I was living. It scared me enough to get me to quit the gang I belonged to and concentrate on finishing high school and getting into college. In order to do this I turned to the Lord for help. Now my life is completely different from then. It was a powerful dream.

Kayla and Lou were both changed by their dreams. The adjustments they made in their lives were a matter of personal insight. Kayla saw clearly the kind of person she had become and where it was leading her. This image was so painful and powerful that it motivated her to make radical changes in her life. Among those who dreamed of dead friends, 45 (32%) thought the dream pointed out something they should do.

The rest of the dreams in this chapter are believed by the dreamers to be messages from dead friends. The messages vary. We'll start with ones that focus on the status of the deceased.

I'm completely healed

The following dream came from Melissa, a fifty-year-old woman who recalled a dream she had about a friend who died from brain tumors. They were both in their twenties at the time and she had the dream one month after her friend died.

> I dreamed I was at a youth fellowship meeting in the church lounge. Suddenly she appeared dressed in white and I could see she had a new body. She was dancing and singing and her body showed no signs of the pain she had suffered or the scars from the tumors that had afflicted her body during her short life. She told me to tell her parents she was fine. She said she had received a complete healing. Then she kissed me and said, "See ya," and I woke up.
>
> The dream assured me that she was free of pain and happy with Jesus. It made me realize how special she was. The dream also meant that I shouldn't get discouraged with the circumstances of this life, for the best is yet to come.

Melissa's religious beliefs were central in her interpretation of her dream, and the dream confirmed the beliefs that she had been taught. Among those who dreamed of dead friends, 65 (46.8%) said the dream convinced them that the dead friends were okay.

In many dreams, there were things that were unexpected and surprising. In the next two dreams, what was surprising was the image of the afterlife.

You need a sponsor

Amy was twenty-seven years old. She related a dream she had about a fifty-four-year-old friend at work who died from AIDS. She had the dream three months later.

> In the dream, I was at work and the phone rang and it was him. He told me he was trying to reach a dead president but got me by mistake. I asked him where he was calling from and he told me he was in Heaven. I asked him how he was doing and he said he was fine. He asked me to tell another coworker

and close friend that he was okay. Then he said he had to go because his sponsor was waiting for him and he had to get off the phone. He hung up. I heard the click and woke up.

The dream made me feel happy. It was good to hear from him and know that he was in Heaven. I was surprised by what he said about making phone calls from there. I wondered if there are phones up in Heaven that you can call other dead people on. I liked that idea. I was also surprised when he mentioned his sponsor. I wondered it we all must have a sponsor or guardian when we first get to Heaven to show us the ropes.

Amy laughed as she talked about the dream. It was clearly comforting, for she believed it really was a message from him. She enjoyed the idea of heavenly phones and was intrigued by the idea of having a sponsor.

You need a ticket

Brittany was an eighteen-year-old whose friend died in an automobile accident. She had the dream one year after he died.

I dreamed I was at a party. It was very crowded but I thought I saw him. I kept working my way through the crowd to see if it was really him. Finally I saw him go out the front door and I followed him. He was just standing there alone, leaning against a pillar. I went up to him and asked him if it was really him and he smiled and said, "Who else?" He looked healthy with no signs of his injuries from the crash. "But you're dead," I said. He just shrugged his shoulders and smiled again. I asked him how it was to be dead. He answered, "It was okay, but you needed a ticket." Then he laughed. (He always used to joke around.)

I woke up feeling strange. The dream was so real, that I thought I had really talked with him. It was eerie, but I was glad to have seen him looking healthy, happy, and still cracking jokes. The dream made me think that death isn't so bad. It's not as scary as I used to think.

Brittany's dream was comforting. It diminished her fears. It also changed her ideas about death.

Still friends

Cynthia was twenty-two years old when she talked about the dream she had two weeks after her friend was killed in a car accident.

I dreamed I was walking down one of the streets in my neighborhood. In the background I could hear a car radio blasting. Soon after hearing that, a car came around the corner. It was my friend's car. He rolled down the window and said to me, "Hey kiddo, you shouldn't be walking out here alone." I was bewildered and asked him if he was alive. He responded with his usual self assuredness, "Of course. 280XZ's never crash." I remained standing next to his car talking to him but I can't remember what else we said.

When I woke up from the dream I was disoriented. In fact, it was so realistic, I got up out of bed to see if his car was in the driveway. It left me really scared and upset. It made me recall different things that he had said to me before he died. For example, every time he saw me walking down the street, he would say that I shouldn't be walking by myself. Moreover, shortly before he died he told my ex-boyfriend that he should get a 280XZ because they never crash. He said both of these things the day before the crash. I think the dream means that I like the idea of always having him around to take care of me like a big brother and that I miss this now that he is gone. I like to imagine him guiding me and protecting me like a guardian angel.

Cynthia is very clear about what she thinks the dream means and she connects the meaning to how she misses his protection and the safe way he made her feel. The realism of the dream convinced her that it meant he was watching over her.

Debra was twenty-five years old. She told of how her high school friend was killed by a drunk driver at the age of twenty-three. She dreamed about her seven months later.

I dreamed I was in my room reading a book. I heard a knock at the door and when I opened it she was standing there. I was shocked because I knew she was dead. She asked me, "May I come in?" I said, "Sure," and stepped aside and she walked in. She looked great, with no signs of the accident. We sat down and she asked me how I was doing. My mind was racing and I said to her, "Fine." Then I said, "If you're dead and in my room talking to me, I must be dead, too." She laughed and said, "Hey, stupid, you're dreaming." After she said this she got up and knocked on my head and yelled, "Hello?" We both laughed and she sat down and asked me how the rest of our friends were taking her death. I told her they were doing as well as could be expected. It was a hit-and-run accident and they hadn't caught the guy. Then she asked me what I was reading, so I showed her my book. She thought it looked like a good read. Then she said she had to leave but that she would like to come back and visit if it was okay. I said it would be fine. Then she slowly disappeared.

I've had other dreams where she comes into my room and visits. Sometimes I ask her advice about some problem I'm having and she tells me what she thinks I should do. The dreams are so real that I forget I'm dreaming and ask her to go to the mall or movies with me. Then when I wake up, I get upset. We had such good times together. I miss her. She had a big influence on my life. I used to model myself after her and now that she's gone, I keep her alive in my dreams. Anyway, my life was getting pretty hectic and I began thinking about her and what she would do in my situation. Soon after that, I began having the dreams. I feel our relationship was special enough for her to be able to come back and visit me.

Debra's dreams began because she missed having her friend around to ask advice from. The dreams provided a way for the relationship to continue. She believes the dreams are a way for her friend to "come back and visit."

Warnings

The next two dreams were warnings to the dreamers. The first one came from Mark, a twenty-nine-year-old man who dreamed of his friend one month after he died of a drug overdose.

> I dreamed we were both hanging out in a park across the street from the apartments where we both lived. I kept asking him why he died. He told me he just couldn't take it any more. I told him I knew what he meant. I was tired of living and I wanted to join him. He grabbed me by the shoulders and shouted in my face, "No! You have responsibilities, things to do." That's when I woke up.
> The dream scared me. It was so real. I could still feel where he had grabbed my shoulders. I was fascinated and wanted the dream to continue so I could talk to him more. I believe my friend came back to tell me that, no matter how hard it gets, I have to keep living and take it one day at a time. As a result of the dream, I was finally able to break my addiction.

The next dream was similar. It came from Scot, a twenty-year-old man whose friend died at the age of seventeen from cardiac arrest after inhaling butane. He first had the dream one week after he died.

> In the dream, I was chasing him with a baseball bat trying to knock the butane can out of his hand. His eyes were totally bugged out and red. He looked really bad. He tried to speak but there was blood in his throat. That was it.
> The dream was so real. I've had the dream many times, usually when I do the sniffing. It's like he won't leave me alone. I couldn't save him and now he's trying to save me. You'd think after all that has happened, I would stop sniffing, but I'm just as stupid as my friend was. It's scary. I know I could die, but it's hard to stop.

Both Mark and Scot had become addicts. Both dreamers believed the dreams were warnings, pointing out adjustments they needed to make in their lives. For Mark, who had tried breaking his crack habit, the dream was powerful enough to get him to stop using. For Scot, who had not tried to stop sniffing, the dream didn't have a strong enough impact.

Invitations to change

Jessica was twenty-three years old when she told the story of her good friend who committed suicide when he was the same age. She had the dream three years after the death and has had it again recently.

> I dreamed I was at a party. I was drunk, and I went into a room, and he was sitting there. I was shocked, because I knew he was dead. I sat down next to him and asked him what he was doing there. And he asked me back what I was doing there! I laughed. Then I asked him, "Why did you do it?" He asked what I was talking about, so I asked again, "Why did you kill yourself?" He was surprised and said, "I didn't." I said, "Yeah, you did; they found you with a shot gun in your apartment and everyone thinks you did it." Then he grabbed my arms and told me that it was my job to tell everyone that he didn't do it. He asked me especially to tell his mother that. Then I woke up.
> It was so real, I woke up shaking. I was confused. The dream left me wondering if what he said was true. I didn't know if I should tell his mother or not. I told my father about the dream and asked him what I should do. He advised me not to tell her. "Some things are better left unsaid," he said, and I agreed. I still wonder whether the dream was a real vision and I question whether his suicide was really a suicide. Maybe my subconscious was telling me that I have something to tell people that can help ease their pain. Or maybe it's just that I don't want to face the fact that he committed suicide, that he shot himself. I wish I knew what really happened that night. The dream also made me look at the way I was living my life. I had the dream around Christmas time when there are lots of parties. It was a rough time. I believe there was a point to my being intoxicated at the party in the dream. I have an illness that requires me to take medication and I shouldn't drink alcohol while taking this drug. That's why holidays are rough. I tend to take one drink and then before I realize it, I'm wasted. The dream made me think of how I could die accidentally, although it could look like something else.

Jessica's dream raised some important issues. She didn't know if she should understand the dream literally and tell her friend's mother that it wasn't a suicide. She chose instead to follow her father's advice, "Some things are better left unsaid." She chose to think that the dream came from her own subconscious. She reflected on the fact that a suicide often has the element of ambiguity. There is often the possibility that at the end, the act was not intentional. Finally, Jessica recognized a connection to her own life with a clear message to change her dangerous behavior. Apparently, she hadn't followed through, so she had the dream again.

April was a thirty-six-year-old woman whose friend died of cancer when she was only eighteen. She had the dream ten years later.

> I dreamed I was sitting outside my home, in my front yard. I heard someone walking and looked up and it was her. She was walking by as if she lived next door. As she passed by my yard, she looked at me and smiled. Then

she said, "Well hello, stranger. I haven't seen you in a long time." And she kept walking without looking back. I tried to catch up with her but she disappeared.

When I woke up, I felt I had done something wrong. I tried to think of what it might have been. Then I remembered how she was an only child and after she died I used to visit her mother a lot because she lived alone. I realized I hadn't visited her in a long time and felt my friend was telling me it was about time to visit her again. The next day I did visit her mother who hugged me and said, "I can't believe it. I was just wondering why you haven't visited in so long. I am so glad to see you. You can't imagine how sad and lonely I've been lately." Ever since that dream, I make sure I visit her mother regularly because I don't want to be called a stranger again!

April believed the dream was a spiritual communication from her dead friend. The message, however, was indirect. April had to discover the meaning that made sense to her.

Goodbyes

Sudden deaths rob the bereaved of the chance to say goodbye. Dreamers often believed their dreams provided an after-death opportunity to do so. Here's an example. Madison was eighteen years old when she related how her friend who was the same age, died in a car accident. Madison had the dream three months later.

In the dream I was asleep until something woke me. When I opened my eyes he was standing next to the bed. He was bruised and bloody, and mangled, hardly recognizable. It was really scary. He reached out and asked me to come with him. I told him I was afraid and he told me I wouldn't die or anything like that. So we got in his car which was a wreck and went for a drive. He started going real fast and I told him to slow down. He laughed and told me not to worry because he couldn't be hurt any more. He slowed down so I wouldn't be so afraid and we started talking about a lot of good times we had in school together. I told him how he was missed by all his friends. He drove me back home and said goodbye and let me out of the car. As I turned toward my house, I woke up.

After first being afraid, the dream made me feel relieved. Our goodbye felt so good. The dream made me remember so many good times with him. I realized how lucky I was to have had such a friend. The dream also made me recognize how precious life is. I believe that we are each given a predetermined amount of time on earth and we'll never know exactly when that time will expire. The dream made me evaluate my priorities and decide what I wanted to do with my life. I've never discussed the dream with anyone before and this was a big relief to finally get out all the feelings.

Final goodbyes are often accompanied with the promise that we'll never forget the person who is dying. Madison was able to say goodbye in the dream, and her dream brought back memories of good times they had together. The dream opened feelings of deep appreciation for the influence her friend had on her life. This led Madison to review her own value system and to resolve to make changes. Madison had many feelings of grief locked inside her. The interview gave her a chance to express some of them.

The next dream is similar but different. It came from Sharon, a twenty-eight-year-old woman whose boyfriend died in a car accident. She had the dream one year later.

> In the dream, I was waiting for him at his house. When I saw him coming, I hid behind the house next door. I was peeking to see where he had gone when he came up behind me and kissed me on the back of my neck. After we hugged, he asked me to walk over to a bench in the backyard with him and we sat down next to each other. He didn't say anything but he rested his head on my shoulder. That was it.
>
> When I woke up, I felt so happy to have been with him again. The dream brought back memories of so many good times we had. It left me feeling lonely. I really missed him. I thought about the dream often and realized that he was telling me our time was over and that I needed to continue on with my life. At the time of the dream, I was very depressed and did not want to start a new relationship. This dream made me realize he still loved me but he was telling me it was okay for me to move on. He was saying goodbye.

Sharon's dream, like Madison's, brought back memories and feelings. They both had something to do with saying goodbye. Each one was offered an opportunity to discover a meaning for the dream. Sharon said she thought about the dream often before its meaning became clear. For her, it was that her friend was saying goodbye to her and giving her permission to "move on."

The last dream about dead friends came from Amber, a twenty-year-old woman whose friend also died in a car accident. She had the dream one year after the death.

> I dreamed I was in the playground that we used to go to when we were kids. I was swinging on the swing-set, and someone was pushing me and talking to me. At first, I heard the voice but I couldn't understand what he was saying. I kind of knew it was him but I didn't. Then I jumped off the swing and fell. He came over and helped me up, and he asked me if I was okay, and I said yes. But he said, "No. Are you okay about my death?" And that's when I looked up and saw that it was him. I was really surprised. I hadn't expected it. We sat and talked for a long time about what happened before he died. We had argued right before his death and so we talked it out and made up.
>
> When we were kids, we used to say if one of us died before the other, to prove there was an afterlife we would come back and say a special sentence, like a secret code. Do you remember Godzilla and Godzooki? He used to tease me all the time saying, "Godzooki doesn't love you." So we decided that if one of us wanted to prove that there was an afterlife then he'd come back through a medium or through a dream or something and would say the sentence, "Godzooki loves you."

In the dream we just talked. He told me he wasn't upset or angry at the person who did this to him, and that I shouldn't be. He told me he loved me and we would be together again someday. We had kind of a crush on each other, and I felt like he was an idiot because he used to talk about other girls and I was sitting right there and I was in love with him. He told me he had always loved me and he just didn't want to ruin our friendship. We were sitting on the swing-set and he told me he had to go but that we would be together again. He told me that everybody is with people they love where he is and sooner or later, we all go back to those we love. I started to cry and he told me not to cry for him because he was with his mother. Finally, he turned to me, hugged me and said, "Godzooki always loved you."

When I woke up, I was crying but was happy. I had been feeling terrible about the argument and I thought I'd never get a chance to make up with him and say goodbye. I thought I'd never get to see him and tell him how I really felt about him. The dream granted all my wishes. It filled me with peace and happiness. Anytime I am feeling depressed, I just recall the dream and I smile and am okay again.

Afterword

A person's life story consists of many stories about relationships. It starts with the tale of the parents who give birth to the child. It continues with stories about siblings, grandparents, aunts and uncles and cousins. Over time there will be narratives about friends and lovers as well as the birth of sons and daughters. Each such story tells of a person's connections with others. It ends with death.

The story of a human life is filled with entrances and exits. Children are born into families. Newborns are introduced to parents, siblings, and other relatives. Friends are introduced for the first time, as are lovers. On the other hand, grown children leave home to go to college, or to get married or to live on their own; friends move far away, and people they care about die.

Deaths are the most difficult exits. With other exits, there is always a hope for reunion. Grown children return home, alienated spouses are reconciled, friends come from afar to visit. When someone dies, however, the departure appears to be final, a dead end.

Grief is the process of adjusting to an exit, especially a death. This book has tried to reveal the elements of grief by presenting the words of different people in grief after a death. They described remembering things about the deceased, some good, some not so good. They told of imagining things about the deceased such as how they would be if they were still alive or what they might be doing in the afterlife. They made clear the emotions they experienced in reaction to the death, emotions like loneliness, anger, guilt, and love. They explained the meaning they found in the relationship leading often to greater appreciation of the deceased. They shared the insights they gained about life, for example, life's uncertainty and sadness. Finally, they made clear their choice to believe that a spiritual transformation had occurred and that the relationship continued.

The exits involved different relationships. There were deaths of grandparents and mothers and fathers; there were brothers and sisters and cousins;

there were spouses and children and friends. All of them were unique. These different relationships affected the quality and extent of the grief.

Each grief is individual for other reasons as well. For example, the cause of death affected the grief. Some deaths were from natural causes but unexpected, while in other cases, the survivors were more prepared for the death. There were tragic deaths of different kinds, suicides, homicides and accidental deaths. The age of the deceased and the age of the bereaved also affected the grief as did their gender. In addition, the religious heritage of the bereaved influenced how the bereaved managed the grief.

There are many ways that people manage grief. Some ways are conscious and deliberate, like planning all the details of a funeral or a memorial service. Others are unconscious, like the dreams that came to the subjects in this study. These dreams about the dead gave the bereaved opportunities to manage their grief.

Their words describe their dreams as well as how the dream helped them adjust to the deaths. Their words are presented in the hope that they will open the mind of the reader to a deeper understanding of grief and the role these kinds of dreams can play in a person's grief. It is also hoped that their words will open the reader's heart to greater compassion for all humans who are in grief.

Appendix: Interview Questions for Dreams about the Dead

1. What was your relationship with the deceased?
2. How old was the deceased when he/she died?
3. What was the cause of death?
4. How long after the death did you have the dream?
5. What exactly happened in the dream?
6. Who were the people in the dream?
7. Where did the dream seem to take place?
8. How did the dream end?
9. How did the dream make you feel?
10. Would any of the following words describe how the dream made you feel? (happy; warm; comforted; encouraged; relieved; peaceful; safe; special; excited; upset; guilty; angry; sad; disappointed; frightened; helpless; jealous; confused; curious; weird; surprised).
11. What did the dream make you think about?
12. Did the dream made you think about any of the following:
    a. that the deceased is really dead
    b. what the deceased suffered
    c. how the deceased died
    d. positive things about the deceased
    e. negative things about the deceased
    f. what was special about the relationship
    g. how much the deceased cared for you
    h. how much you miss the deceased
    i. regrets over things not done
    j. what if the deceased were still alive
    k. the funeral
    l. the direction in which your life is going
    m. what is really important in life
    n. life after death
    o. something you should do
    p. a living relationship

     q. your own mortality
     r. the mortality of someone else
     s. the value of being alive
     t. the deceased is okay
     u. the deceased is watching over you.
13. What was surprising about the dream?
14. Besides the death, what else in your life might have contributed to the dream?
15. If the dream were the answer to a question, what would the question be?
16. What does this dream tell you about yourself?

Endnotes

1. See Stephen La Berge's *Lucid Dreams*. (NY: Ballantine, 1986)
2. Souvay, Charles. "The Interpretation of Dreams," in the *Catholic Encyclopedia*: Vol V. http://www.newadvent.org/cathen/05154a.htm 2003
3. For example, George Slater's, *Bringing Dreams to Life: Learning to Interpret Your Dreams* (New York: Paulist Press, 1995)
4. *After Death Communication*. (St. Paul, MN: Llewellyn Publications, 1997) 142.
5. *The Interpretation of Dreams* (New York: The Modern Library, 1950; originally copyrighted 1938)
6. *Dreams*, translated by R. F. C. Hull (Princeton Univ. Press, 1974)
7. Calvin S. Hall & Vernon J. Nordby, *The Individual and His Dreams*. (New York: Mentor Books, 1972)
8. Robert L. Van de Castle, *Our Dreaming Mind*. (New York: Ballantine Press, 1994), 208
9. *Dreams: Discovering Your Inner Teacher*. (Minneapolis: Winston Press, 1983) 42.
10. See Kenneth Kramer's *Death Dreams* (New York: Paulist Press, 1993)
11. Erich Lindemann, "The Symptomology and Management of Acute Grief," *American Journal of Psychiatry* 101 (1944)
12. See J. William Worden's *Grief Counseling and Grief Therapy: A Handbook for the Mental Health Practitioners*, 3rd ed. (New York: Springer, 2002) and Therese A. Rando's *Treatment of Complicated Mourning*. (Champaign, IL: Research Press, 1993).
13. Margaret Stroebe, "Coping with Bereavement: A Review of the Grief Work Hypothesis" *Omega: Journal of Death and Dying* 26, no. 1 (1992-93); Torill Christine Lindstrom, "'It Ain't Necessarily So': Challenging Mainstream Thinking about Bereavement," *Family & Community Health* 25, no. 1 (2002)
14. "Relearning the World: Making and Finding Meanings," in *Meaning Reconstructiion and the Experience of Loss*, Neimeyer, R. A., (ed.) (Washington D.C.: American Psychological Association, 2001) 42
15. Robert A. Neimeyer, ed. "Introduction," *Meaning Reconstruction and the Experience of Loss*. (Washington D.C.: American Psychological Association, 2001) 2-4.
16. Cassirer, Ernst. *An Essay on Man*. (New Haven: Yale Univ. Press, 1944)
17. *Attachment and Loss: Vol. 3: Loss, Sadness, and Depression*. (New York: Basic Books, 1982)

18. "Through a Glass Darkly: Images of the Dead in Dreams," *Omega: Journal of Death and Dying.* 24 (1991-1992): 97-101.
19. *The Dream Messenger: How Dreams of the Departed Bring Healing Gifts.* (New York: Simon and Schuster, 1997)
20. *Grief Dreams: How they heal us after the death of a loved one.* (San Francisco, CA: Jossey-Bass, 2005).
21. Miller, M., Stinson, L. & Soper, B. "The Use of Dream Discussions in Counseling," *The Personnel and Guidance Journal.* 61 (1982): 142-150.
22. Neimeyer, Robert A. & Hogan, Nancy "Quantitative or Qualitative? Measurement Issues in the Study of Grief." In *Handbook of Bereavement Research: Consequences, Coping, and Care,* ed. Stroebe, Margaret S., Hansson, Robert O., Stroebe, Wolfgang, & Schut, Henk. (Washington D.C.: American Psychological Association, 2001) 105-6
23. *After Death Communication*, 168. See also *Grief Counseling and Grief Therapy,* and the *Treatment of Complicated Mourning.*
24. "Exploring Religious America: A Poll Conducted for *Religion & Ethics Newsweekly* and *U.S. News & World Report* by Mitofsky International and Edison Media Research, March 26 – April 4, 2002, <htpp://www.pbs.org/wnet/religionandethics/week534/specialreport.html> (8July 2005)
25. *After Death Communication,* 154.
26. "An Integrative Model of Grief." *Death Studies,* 19, (1995): 337-364
27. See Tony Walter's *On Bereavement: The Culture of Grief.* (Philadelphia: Open University Press, 1999)
28. See Erna Furman's, *A Child's Parent Dies: Studies in Childhood Bereavement.* (New Haven CT: Yale University Press, 1974)
29. See Christine Longaker's *Facing Death and Finding Hope: A Guide to the Emotional and Spiritual Care of the Dying.* (New York: Doubleday, 1997)
30. See Geddes MacGregor's *Images of Afterlilfe: From Antiquity to Modern Times.* (New York: Paragon, 1992)
31. See F. Walsh & Monica McGoldrick's (eds) *Living Beyond Loss.* (New York: Norton, 1991)
32. See Earl Grollman's ed. *Explaining Death to Children.* (Boston: Beacon Press, 1967)
33. Van der Wal, Jan. "The Aftermath of Suicide: A Review of Empirical Evidence." *Omega: Journal of Death and Dying* 20, no.2 (1989-90): 149-171.
34. Schneidman, Edwin S., *Deaths of Man.* (New York: Quadrangle Books, 1973) 81-90.
35. *Treatment of Complicated Mourning* (Champaign IL.: Research Press, 1993) 112.
36. *On Death and Dying.* (New York: Prentice-Hall, 1969)
37. See Dennis Klass' *Parental Grief: Solace and Resolution.* (New York: Springer, 1988)
38. Klass, Dennis, "Solace and Immortality: Bereaved Parents' Continuing Bond with their Children." In *The Path Ahead: Readings in Death and Dying*, ed. DeSpelder and Strickland (Mountain View, CA: Mayfield, 1995) 246-259.

Bibliography

Attig, Thomas. *The Heart of Grief: Death and the Search for Lasting Love.* New York: University Press, 2000.

Barrett, Deirdre. "Through a Glass Darkly: Images of the Dead in Dreams," *Omega: Journal of Death and Dying.* 24 (1991-1992): 97-101.

Doka, Kenneth J. (Ed.) *Disenfranchised Grief,* Lexington, MA: Lexington Books, 1989.

Faraday, Ann. *Dream Power.* New York: Berkeley Books, 1980.

Garfield, Patricia. *The Dream Messenger: How Dreams of the Departed Bring Healing Gifts.* New York: Simon and Schuster, 1997.

Hall, Calvin S. & Vernon J. Nordby. *The Individual and His Dreams.* New York: Mentor Books, 1972.

Jung, Carl. *Memories, Dreams, Reflections.* New York: Random House, 1961.

Kastenbaum, Robert & B. K. Kastenbaum (Eds.), *Encyclopedia of Death.* Phoenix: Oryx, 1989.

Klass, Dennis. *Parental Grief Solace and Resolution.* New York: Springer, 1988.

Klass, Dennis, Phyllis R. Silverman, and Steven Nickman, eds. *Continuing New Understandings of Grief.* Washington, D.C.: Taylor & Francis, 1996.

Kramer, Kenneth. *Death Dreams.* New York: Paulist Press, 1993.

LaBerge, Stephen. *Lucid Dreams.* New York: Ballantine Press, 1986.

LaGrand, Louis. *After Death Communication.* St. Paul, MN: Llewellyn Publications, 1997.

MacGregor, Geddes. *Images of Afterlife: From Antiquity to Modern Times.* New York: Paragon, 1992.

Moody, Raymond. *Reunions: Visionary Encounters with Departed Loved Ones.* New York: Villard Books, 1994.

Neimeyer, Robert A. (ed.) *Meaning Reconstructiion and the Experience of Loss.* Washington D.C.: American Psychological Association, 2001.

Parkes, Colin Murray. *Bereavement: Studies of Grief in Adult Life,* New York: Routledge, 2001.

Rando, Theresa A. *Grieving: How to Go on Living When Someone You Love Dies.* Lexington, MA: Lexington Books, 1988.

Rando, Theresa. *Loss and Anticipatory Grief.* Lexington, MA: Lexington Books. 1986.

Reid, Clyde H. *Dreams: Discovering your Inner Teacher.* Minneapolis: Winston Press, 1983.

Slater, George. *Bringing Dreams to Life: Learning to Interpret Your Dreams.* New York: Paulist Press, 1995

Stroebe, Margaret S., W. Stroebe, & R. Hansson (eds.). *Handbook of Bereavement.* Cambridge: Cambridge University Press, 1993.

Stroebe, Margaret S, R. Hansson, W. Stroebe, & H. Schut. (eds.) *Handbook of Bereavement Research: Consequences, Coping, and Care.* Washington, D.C.: American Psychological Association, 2001.

Van de Castle, Robert L. *Our Dreaming Mind.* New York: Ballantine Press, 1994.

Von Fraanz, Marie-Louise. *On Dreams and Death.* Boston: Shambala, 1986.

Walsh, Francis & Monica McGoldrick (eds) *Living Beyond Loss.* New York: Norton, 1991.

Walter, Tony. *On Bereavement: The Culture of Grief.* Philadelphia: Open University Press, 1999.

Worden, J. William. *Grief Counseling & Grief Therapy,* 2nd ed., New York: Springer Publishing Co., 1991.

Wray, T. J. Ann Proce. *Grief Dreams: How they heal us after the death of a loved one.* (San Francisco, CA: Jossey-Bass, 2005.

Index